MORE MONEY FOR BEER AND TEXTBOOKS

A Financial Guide for Today's Canadian Student

KYLE PREVOST · JUSTIN BOUCHARD

MORE MONEY FOR BEER AND TEXTBOOKS

A Financial Guide for Today's Canadian Student

YOUNG AND THRIFTY PUBLICATIONS
2013

First Edition, 2013.
First Printing, 2013.

The text of this book is composed
in Adobe Caslon Pro and Helvetica,
with the display set in BigNoodleTitling;
the subtitle and cover use Palatino Linotype.

The cover was designed by Sherwin Soy
and refined by Forrest Adam Sumner.

The cover of this book is acid-free; the pages are acid-free and lignin-free; both the cover and the pages meet all of the American National Standards Institute's criteria for archival-quality paper.

ISBN 978-0-9917482-0-4

Printed and Bound
in the United States of America,
by Lightning Source, Inc.,
1246 Heil Quaker Boulevard,
La Vergne, Tennessee, 37086.

To our parents,
for teaching us how to fish
and for giving us more than a
few catches of the day as well.

ACKNOWLEDGEMENTS

WE'D like to thank all of the people who made this book happen. It may sound cliché, but More Money for Beer and Textbooks could not have become a reality without the help of our many friends and the personal-finance blogging community, who acted as our sounding-board.

Our amazing editor and publishing wizard, Forrest Adam Sumner, also was essential to our efforts. He not only did basic copyediting and proofreading, but also provided excellent advice, spent hours on necessary research and fact-checking, wrote much original material, designed these pages, produced the graph and some promotional material, prepared everything for print, and refined Sherwin Soy's great design for the cover. Any shortcomings remaining after Mr. Sumner's work are entirely our responsibility.

A big thanks as well to our parents, for supporting us in all our endeavours.

To the students whose energy motivates us every day: We salute you!

Finally, we would be remiss if we did not thank our significant others, Molly and Patricia, for putting up with our antics and for loving us nonetheless. For everything you do, ladies, Thank You!

CONTENTS

INTRODUCTION
WHY THIS ISN'T A WASTE OF YOUR TIME

CONGRATULATIONS! The fact that you have opened up a book that is supposed to help you with this financial stuff means that you are more prepared for your post-secondary education than the vast majority of students out there. Whether you are in high school, college, or university, taking a few minutes to prepare yourself financially by reading this book will save you a lot of headaches later on. We should admit right up front that it would have been pretty difficult to get us to crack a book like this when we were young adults—so cheers to you for making the effort!

Almost every self-help book we have ever forced ourselves to read has been terribly dry and boring. We did our best to ensure that MORE MONEY FOR BEER AND TEXTBOOKS didn't turn out that way. We also know how much of a drag it can be to pick up something that's supposed to help you, only to have it look suspiciously like a textbook and weigh enough to do bench-press repetitions with. When we sat down to write this personal-finance guide, we aimed to cut out all the fluff and simply give Canadian students some realistic, honest ways to keep a little cash in their pockets as they went through school. It isn't anything too wild or ambitiously crazy; we don't advise you never to spend a nickel or to sacrifice your whole life on the altar of frugality. Instead, this is merely a simple look at post-secondary life, written by two guys who wish they had known then what they know now.

When we were eighteen, we didn't have the faintest clue what acronyms like *RESP* meant or how to save money on taxes. We can honestly say that if either of us had read this book before entering post-secondary education his bank account would have had *at least* $5,000 more in it at graduation—and there's an argument to be made for much more money than that. We think that's why this book is a pretty decent deal. For under $20 and a couple hours of your time, you get tips on how to save thousands of dollars on everything from tax returns to scholarships and the bar scene. This isn't a catch-all book that has the same generic advice that you could find in 1,001 newspapers, magazines, and libraries. This is a comprehensive guide written specifically for Canadian students (and, to some extent, their parents). There is also a useful bonus: it's not painful to read, because we're not trying to show everyone how big our vocabulary is and how smart we are.

WHO ARE THESE GUYS, AND WHY DID THEY GET TOGETHER FOR THIS BOOK?

So why the heck should you listen to us? Good question. We aren't accountants or business types, and we definitely don't have *all* the answers. What we do have is plenty of experience dealing with the world of post-secondary education from all angles—and a passion for helping students out.

Inevitably, in the rapidly changing world that our youth are thrown into today, much of their future hinges on their success in post-secondary education. Before we decided we should get grown-up jobs, few would have described us as two guys who were going to write a financial guide of any sort. We didn't always make the right decisions, and we aren't millionaires. We did have a ton of fun, learn from our mistakes, and come out way ahead of the "average" Canadian student (at least according to the "new norm" debt levels we read about every day).

The reason why you got two brains for the price of one when you bought More Money for Beer and Textbooks is that we believe our experiences complement each other very well. Not only did we take slightly different paths as students and consequently learn different lessons, but also our careers approach helping young adults from different angles. Justin helps students thrive in a post-secondary setting as the dean of residence at St. John's College, at the University of Manitoba, while Kyle prepares somewhat younger students to achieve their goals and dreams at Birtle Collegiate high school. Together, we were able to produce what we believe is a truly authoritative book that can be applied to a wide range of backgrounds, perspectives, and ages. Throughout the rest of this book, we'll usually talk about ourselves jointly, using "we", "us", and similar words. Occasionally, we'll present a perspective or experience that fits only one or the other of us, not both; in those cases, we'll talk about "Kyle" and "Justin" separately and in the third person. We realize this might be slightly awkward to read, but, hey, "#firstworldproblems", as the kids say these days.

Why Write a Book?

We wrote this book for two reasons.

First of all, we wrote it to help post-secondary students like our eighteen-year-old selves and almost all of the people we went to school with—students who, really, have no idea about financial reality, because they weren't taught much about it in high school, and whose parents didn't know much about anything at all when their kids were thirteen to seventeen (it's funny how your parents seem to get smarter as you get older).

Second, we realized that there's nothing else like More Money for Beer and Textbooks on the market. Sure, you can find books written for American students, or books written ten years ago for a student body that's much different from that which exists today. You can even find some resources that are written for some imaginary student who gets straight *A*s, has the ideal job, is perfectly organized, and has never touched alcohol before. In our experience, those books are of little use to the students we interact with every day. If we can help people avoid the mistakes we made and easily learn the lessons we and our friends had to learn the hard way, then that is something to feel pretty good about!

Personal-finance gurus will tell you that trying to experience certain types of entertainment while in post-secondary schooling is the path to financial ruin. While there is a kernel of truth in that belief when those efforts are taken to extremes, we are prime examples of the fact that you do not have to choose between living like a monk and being $100,000 in debt when you get out of school. That's why we believe we're offering something that no one else has offered—a viable guide to having fun in school without breaking the bank, written by two guys who have learned from their mistakes but are still young enough to remember why they made them.

Making *a few* dumb choices while you're in college or university can mean a handful of expensive lessons learned. Making *a series* of dumb choices while you're in school can lead to a massive pit of crippling debt lying in wait for you after you take off the cap and gown. We aren't trying to scare you, but you should be aware of the tough reality that students and young graduates face in today's world. Rather than dread leaving your cocoon of higher education, why not plan for it and be prepared to hit the ground running, instead of being held back by the ball-and-chain of student debt? Post-secondary education absolutely can catapult you ahead in life; but it can also throw you right into a chaotic world of credit-card debt, student loans, frustrated landlord parents, and limited job prospects—if you allow it to. We're not trying to be melodramatic here, but we don't think it's a stretch to say that today's students have it harder on average than any other group has had it for a long time. Let's face it: students need all the help they can get.

If earning a diploma or a degree while paying for it at the same time looks like a mountain that gets higher every day, one with a summit you will never reach, you should take comfort in knowing you're far from the first person to feel this way and you won't be the last. We sincerely hope this book makes life just a little bit easier for you and helps you understand a few things most of us have had to learn from the school of hard knocks.

CHAPTER ONE

HOW MUCH WILL SCHOOL COST . . . AND IS IT EVEN WORTH IT?

BEFORE we get into saving money and how to become an expert on the finer points of beer consumption, we probably should address the number-one question on the minds of students bound for post-secondary education. (It's also on the minds of their parents.) ***How much is this going to cost?***

We won't lie to you. Today is not an easy time to be a young person, or the supportive parent of a young person. It seems that not a week goes by without a new study coming out that talks about the record levels of student debt or the rapidly rising costs of tuition. The truth is that it's extremely difficult to pinpoint exactly how much school will cost for your specific situation. Depending on what sort of post-secondary education you want, where you want to go to school, and what sort of lifestyle you plan to live while studying, the answer to the overall $$$ question varies quite a bit.

A survey of students across Canada done by *RateSupermarket.ca* in September 2012 estimates that a student leaving high school today will pay an average total cost of $78,817 for a basic four-year degree if living away from home. Here's how that breaks down:

Average Canadian university tuition for four years	$21,464
Expenses (books, transportation, entertainment, housing, meal plan, etc.)	45,520
Interest on average university-graduate debt	11,833
Total	**$78,817**

The numbers are a little easier to stomach if Mom and Dad don't mind having a roommate for four more years:

Average Canadian university tuition for four years	$21,464
Expenses (books, transportation, entertainment, etc.)	11,520
Interest on average university-graduate debt	2,451
Total	**$35,435**

By comparison, here are the averages for *two*-year college diplomas. First, not living with your parents:

Average Canadian college tuition for two years	$5,356
Expenses (books, transportation, entertainment, housing, meal plan, etc.)	22,760
Interest on average university-graduate debt	1,991
Total	**$30,107**

A two-year college diploma if you live with your parents:

Average Canadian college tuition for two years	$5,356
Expenses (books, transportation, entertainment, etc.)	5,760
Interest on average university-graduate debt	244
Total	**$11,360**

The interest was calculated from Canadian average student-debt levels, an average starting income of $39,523 a year (with five percent of it going toward debt repayment), and an extremely optimistic three-percent annual interest rate. You may have noticed that the interest costs are lower for students living at home: this is because the lower cost of living with your parents means that you need to borrow less and therefore can race faster to the end of paying those pesky interest charges. If you're a little rusty on what interest is and how it works, see the beginning of CHAPTER 7 for a quick refresher. Also of note: the average university student in Canada these days takes *fourteen years* to pay off student debt.

While these numbers might surprise parents who have fond memories of their $1,000 tuition and plentiful summer jobs for all who wanted them, they actually weren't surprising to us recent grads. Moreover, the sizeable difference in overall cost between a college education and a university education presents an interesting cost–benefit scenario to aspiring young Canadians.

Looking for a general itemized breakdown? Here are our estimated ranges for the different categories in a typical Canadian student's annual budget today. Remember that this doesn't take into account one-time costs, such as a computer, furniture, and a car—and these are the costs for just one year:

	Expense	Minimum	Maximum
Room and board	Rent and	$5,000	$6,000
	Food	3,000	3,000
	Utilities, Internet, and cable	1,000	1,500
	Or		
	Residence and meal plan	5,500	12,000
	Plus		
Edu. and Misc.	Tuition and compulsory fees	4,000	40,000
	Textbooks	200	1,200
	School supplies	100	1,000
	Gym pass	500	800
	Entertainment and beer money	1,200	?
	Plus		
Transport.	Transit pass	750	750
	Or		
	Personal-vehicle costs (*in addition* to purchase price)	3,000	6,000
	Grand total	**$12,250+**	**$62,200+**

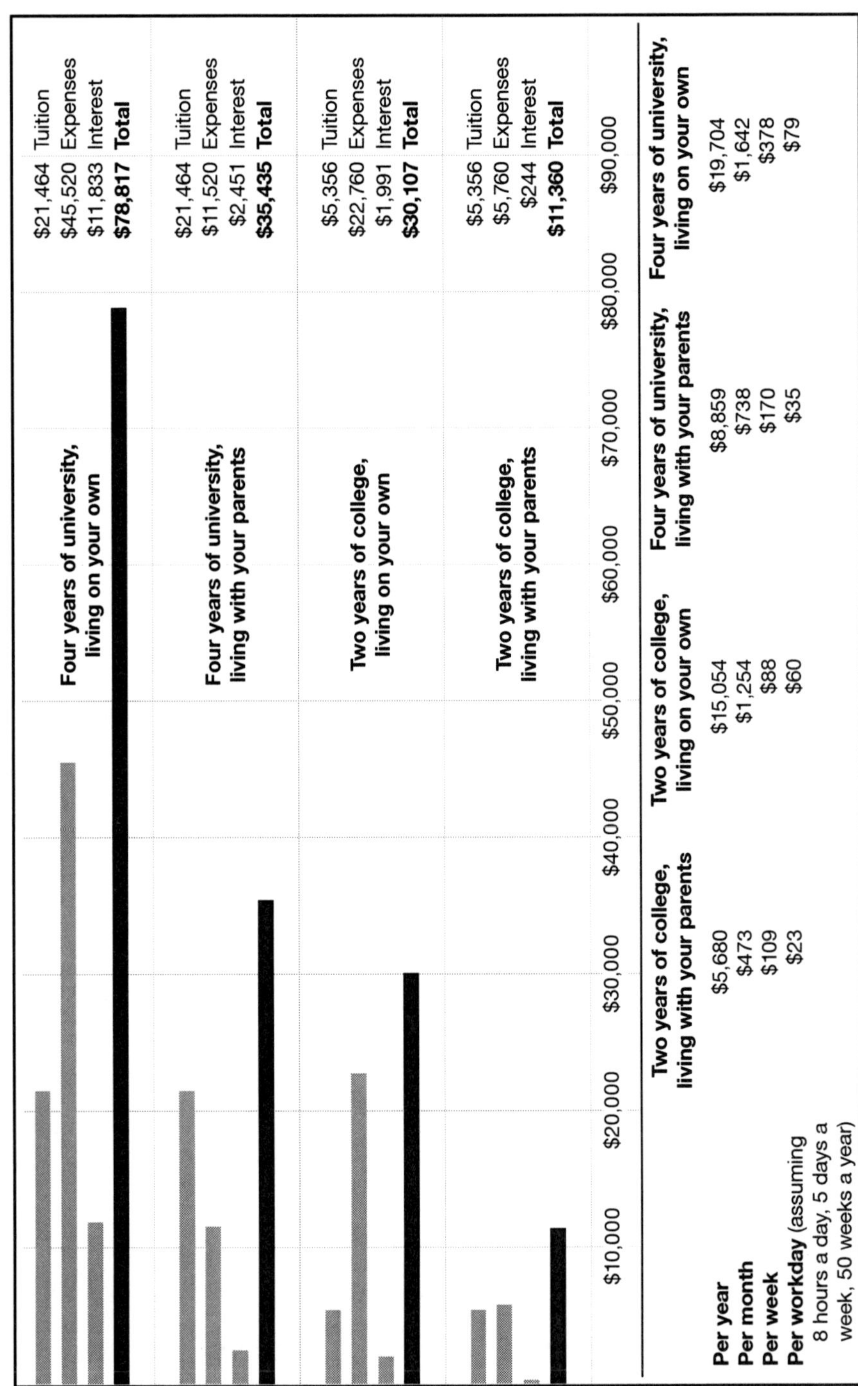

	Two years of college, living with your parents	Two years of college, living on your own	Four years of university, living with your parents	Four years of university, living on your own
Per year	$5,680	$15,054	$8,859	$19,704
Per month	$473	$1,254	$738	$1,642
Per week	$109	$88	$170	$378
Per workday (assuming 8 hours a day, 5 days a week, 50 weeks a year)	$23	$60	$35	$79

As you can see, depending on a few key choices, your bottom line can differ quite a bit. For example, do your tuition and fees cost you $4,000—or $40,000? The most expensive option in the table on page 9 costs more than five times as much as the cheapest. Our personal estimate for attending one of Canada's universities away from home and pursuing an undergraduate degree is roughly $20,000 a year—approaching $100,000 for four years. Rob Carrick, the prominent personal-finance guru for *The Globe and Mail*, recently quoted a similar number as he looked ahead to his eighteen-year-old son's life after high school.

How did we get to this point in Canadian society, where everyone tells youth that they should be pursuing a post-secondary education but those same adults seem not to have many original ideas about climbing a financial mountain that grows taller every year? Well, we actually got there incrementally. While many Baby Boomers are fond of pointing out that a litre of milk and a carton of eggs also don't cost what they did back when the Boomers were in school, the math simply doesn't support the argument that the cost of post-secondary education has risen merely at the rate of general inflation.

A 2012 report from the Canadian Centre for Policy Alternatives shows that since 1990 the average university tuition and compulsory fees for Canadian undergraduate students have risen at an astounding rate: an average of 6.2 percent annually. Those yearly rises took place over a period when the rate of general inflation was only about one third the rate at which tuition and fees were rising. The study states that the average tuition and fees for a full course load today are $6,186 for a school year, and that number is expected to climb to a stifling $7,330 by 2015. The raw arithmetic that Mr. Carrick points to in one of his columns, titled "2012 vs. 1984: Young Adults Really Do Have It Harder Today", shows that, if the rise in university tuition and fees had matched general inflation, the $1,000 tuition levels he enjoyed as a student in 1984 would have risen to just $2,028 today. In reality, those costs are more than three times as high.

If the costs of college and university are rising much faster than general expenses or wages, one might expect fewer Canadians to be pursuing post-secondary studies. The interesting truth is that more Canadians than ever before are attending classes after high school. Perhaps it is the nature of the new world economy, or it could be simply that today's generation has been coached to believe that they *must* pursue post-secondary education no matter what. Whatever the reason, the fact is that, with more and more people paying larger and larger sums of money to obtain post-secondary credentials, something has to give. The chief candidate for what might eventually burst is the bubble that's being inflated year after year—that of student debt. As of September 2011, there were over $22-billion in outstanding student loans in circulation: that's roughly equivalent to the combined annual government budgets for all four Atlantic provinces! While student debt is tax-deductible, and interest rates at all-time lows have made payments easier to stomach in recent years, the drag that a large debt burden can put on our young adults is substantial and nothing to ignore.

So, what's a student to do? Youth unemployment rates across Canada hover around fourteen percent, and consequently the battle for entry-level jobs has rarely been this desperate. Young people today realize that, in order to compete in the global marketplace, they need some kind of training after high school—but they aren't really told how to get it or even what training might be most advantageous. Then we generally throw them to the wolves and pray that they come out with less debt than the last generation took out *to buy a house*. Finally, more and more of our students have grown up in environments that prize building kids' self-esteem above all else, meaning they're simply not prepared to deal with the financial realities of an increasingly competitive world.

Believe it or not, there is good news. By reading this book, you're already ahead of the game and are well on your way to navigating the treacherous financial jungle young Canadians face today!

The other news you should find encouraging is that attending post-secondary schooling is still generally a great deal, even though costs are skyrocketing. The financial benefits of attaining a college diploma or a university degree are well documented. Paul Davidson, President of the Association of Universities and Colleges of Canada, has highlighted census information showing the average lifetime earnings of someone with an undergraduate degree will be about *$1.4-million* more than those of someone without a post-secondary degree. Even the average college graduate's lifetime earnings will be about $400,000 more than those of the person without a post-secondary degree. We are a little dubious as to how large the gap is between college diplomas and university degrees in that information, but the principle that a post-secondary education still holds a lot of value is consistent across every study we've read. Davidson goes on to say that, since the economic shakedown that began in 2008, there have been more than 300,000 *new jobs created* for university graduates—and there's been a *loss* of 430,000 jobs for those without post-secondary education. With the disappearance of so many blue-collar manufacturing jobs, there's little doubt we're moving quickly to a more information-based economy—and this will largely benefit certain types of post-secondary education, regardless of the initial cost of that education.

While there is no denying the fact that students today face an uphill battle, it is not exactly *Mission: Impossible* to get your degree while you keep your overall debt figure low. It will require some tough choices and a little bit of effort in order to get your financial house in order, but the juice is definitely worth the squeeze. Many students stumble through their late teens and early twenties in some sort of student-loan-fuelled, lifestyle-inflating haze. They believe that a budget is more confusing than advanced calculus, and debt becomes some imaginary concept to be dealt with in a faraway land called "The Future". If you can manage to learn and execute a few key tips found within these pages, they can make a substantial difference in your getting out of school on good financial terms and in keeping you out of the "Look at How Much Student Debt I Have" features that newspapers love so much these days.

Chapter 1 Summary

- A post-secondary education costs a lot of money—especially if you decide to move out of your parents' place to attend school (roughly $20,000 per year in that case).
- Tuition is rising at a rate much quicker than that of general inflation. This means that school is likely to take up an ever growing portion of the average personal or family budget as the years go by.
- Canadian students are taking on more debt than ever before, and the amount they owe is increasing rapidly.
- A post-secondary education is still an excellent investment, and will stay that way in an information-based economy.

CHAPTER TWO

WHEREVER I LAY MY HEAD IS HOME

WHILE living in residence might mean having the time of your life, and getting an apartment with a couple of close friends may be the experience you planned all through high school, the undeniable fact as far as your wallet is concerned is that your mom and dad are the best roommates in the world. Regardless of the glorious lifestyle that college movies depict, the statistics simply don't lie. The *RateSupermarket.ca* survey results mentioned in CHAPTER 1 vividly illustrate the huge difference that increased living expenses can make in the total cost of an education. The easiest way to save $45,000 while you're going to university, or $11,000 while you're at college, is simply to live at home.

We know this probably isn't what most of you want to hear: If you're lucky enough to live close to a decent post-secondary option and you and your parents can co-exist around each other without spontaneously combusting, it's hard to justify not living at home if your folks are up to it. Even if you have to pay a little bit of rent in order to sweeten the deal, chances are it's still a ridiculously good financial move.

Few students have any clue how much money their parents spend on relatively small individual purchases for the household and how quickly they all add up. Such things as toiletries, supplies for laundry and cleaning and the kitchen, food itself, and dozens of other incidental items that used to appear magically in the house when you lived with your parents can cost you a much bigger portion of your budget than you thought. This doesn't even take into account such things as borrowing the family car a few times a week instead of owning your own vehicle; using Mom and Dad's furniture, computer, and printer; and other one-time costs you'll have to figure out how to pay for if you move away.

We loved the independence we each experienced when we'd moved out of our parents' places for school. We believe the decision to move away from home and to live on campus played a large part in making both of us who we are today. At the same time, we didn't have much choice, because we grew up in rural areas too far from any campus to commute.

Still, you can't ignore the effect that your choice of where to live can have on your wallet. Remember, for living in residence, we're talking about at least $5,500 for an eight-month year: that's at least $687.50 a month, or at least $22.59 every single day, that you have to spend—or *get to save*—depending on the choice you make.

Ultimately, it comes down to your priorities and how much you are willing to sacrifice for them. "Complete" freedom and the experiences that can come with independent living are extremely attractive and valuable . . . but so is a stack of *four hundred and fifty* $100 bills (which offer another form of freedom).

ON CAMPUS VS. OFF CAMPUS

It's tough for us not to be biased when it comes to discussing student housing options. Although we both lived off campus at some point while going through school, we agree that living on campus was essential not only to the lives we enjoyed as students but also to our futures. We first met many of our lifelong friends while living on campus—and Kyle met his better half there. In fact, we could probably write a whole book just on the benefits of living in residence. But, in the interest of keeping things short and sweet (two things we are decidedly not), we'll simply refer you to Justin's blog, *MyUniversityMoney.com*, in case you want to take a more in-depth look at what makes on-campus living so special for many people (and what to avoid if you want to graduate at some point!).

Much of the debate about living on campus and living off can be quantified in dollars and cents. But there are several important considerations that don't show up on a balance sheet. Before we boil things down to the lowest common denominator (money), here are a few points to help you decide which type of housing is better for you:

1. Living with other young people is a fantastic experience—which you will hate about once a week. Being surrounded by hundreds of students at relatively the same stage in life is ideal for forming lasting connections and consistently having a blast. Being surrounded by hundreds of young people also requires a sacrifice of privacy, overall control, and noise standards. For some people, that sacrifice just isn't worth it. For us, it was a small price to pay.

2. Living on campus can really help you academically. You should miss fewer classes because you're just a ten-minute walk from anywhere on campus. Also nearby are the library and all the other technical support that a campus offers. Many studies state that, for the average student, living on campus makes the transition from high school to post-secondary study easier.

3. Living on campus can cripple you academically. Why? There is always a party somewhere on campus. Sunday night? Been there. Tuesday afternoon? What better way to celebrate the first Tuesday of the week! At some point, either you learn to organize yourself and balance out the opportunities for fun with a little TLC for your GPA, or you crash and burn before moving out

of residence. The good thing is that this critical choice is entirely yours to make.

4. Some people believe that residence food is gross and that there is no selection. This was not our experience, and as a couple of big guys we appreciated the large serving-sizes. Another popular argument is that food plans are overpriced at universities. While this may be true (especially for smaller eaters), don't forget that when you live off campus you need to worry about food preparation and cleaning the kitchen. For those of you who tend to let food go bad, or who find yourselves often going out for fast food because you don't have the energy to make supper, this fact alone can make it worthwhile to live in residence.

5. In addition to the obvious monetary benefits of not commuting, there is also a huge time factor. We place a very high premium on freeing up our time and being efficient with our day—so spending a couple of hours every day waiting for and then taking a bus is not our thing. Think about the fact that all of that waiting adds up to over 700 hours every year—700 hours that you could be using on something productive or fun!

6. Living on campus puts you right at the heart of a diverse selection of extracurricular activities. There is no better place to be if you want to participate in a drama club, choir, intramurals, dance lessons, or the debate team. Most people who commute don't take advantage of nearly as many of these offerings, because it's just not as convenient.

If you find yourself saying, "Yeah, sure, all that stuff is fine and good—but which one takes a bigger chunk out of my bank account?" just read on for a summary of the financial differences between living on campus and off. While most people who are supposed to know about this stuff will tell you that living on campus costs more, that is not entirely true. Depending on your personal circumstances, one option might cost slightly more than the other; but overall we've found that they usually come out pretty close to equal. The University of Windsor has a very thorough cost comparison at *uwindsor.ca/residence/comparing-costs.* Here are the major considerations as we see them:

1. The monthly cost of on-campus housing will probably be higher than that of off-campus options, but by the same token many students don't want to live in the same area during the summer where they live during the school year. Many students move away in May to pursue lucrative work opportunities, and others move back home for various reasons. In those situations, the eight-month on-campus contracts are often the best option available. When you talk to landlords about drawing up a contract for only the eight-month school year, don't be surprised if they stare at you in confused disbelief. Rentals are almost always signed for twelve months at a time; and, given the lack of rental vacancies close to Canadian campuses, this isn't likely to change. So, when you're comparing costs, consider whether you will or won't leave town for the summer: if you will be gone all summer, ask yourself about the wisdom of continuing to pay rent for four months on an apartment you're not even setting foot in.

2. The question of how many roommates (if any) you're sharing housing costs with can radically affect your budget. If you choose to live with a roommate in residence, it will cut your costs down substantially (although we wouldn't recommend this to a lot of people). The same logic applies to various off-campus arrangements. Some of our pals saved tons of money by renting a five-bedroom house together and splitting the rent five ways. Other people crave the privacy of living by themselves or with one roommate with whom they are particularly close. Make sure to apply the relevant rates for your specific situation.

3. As we mentioned before, living off campus means increased transportation costs. If you go to a school where a public-transit

fee is built in to your tuition, this may not affect you much anyway. If you plan to use a personal vehicle, though, these costs can be substantial. You may need to compare specific parking costs for on-campus and off-campus scenarios at your school.

4. Many people claim that purchasing their own food and cooking for themselves saves them money over the inflated prices of student meal plans. We're not sure this should be as widely accepted as it is, but we've talked to many people who are absolutely sure about this. Maybe the two of us just aren't that good at grocery shopping and cooking.

5. Living on campus gives you access to a ton of cheap to free entertainment options. Just by being around so many young and energetic people and piggy-backing on their creativity, you can have a great time that doesn't involve a debit or credit card. One example is the crazy campus-wide games of Capture the Flag we used to play whenever someone got the motivation to round everyone up. If you haven't sprinted across your campus at full speed playing a child's game at one o'clock in the morning, you simply haven't lived.

6. Before we give you some tips on how to save money on furnishing a place (coming up in just a moment), don't forget that most residence rooms come fully furnished—and there isn't room to put anything else in them even if you want to. Although it might take you a few days to get used to the meagre square footage that you are allotted when you live on campus, there is no better way to practice this "minimalist lifestyle" that has become all the rage among personal-finance gurus everywhere. To put it simply, you can't spend money on furniture, 103 pairs of shoes, pets, and a big-screen TV if you don't have space for furniture, 101 pairs of shoes, pets, and a big-screen TV.

7. When comparing the costs of on-campus and off-campus housing, remember to "compare apples to apples" and budget for ev-

erything that on-campus housing charges you for up front: items such as utilities (monthly costs plus initial hookup fees), cable, Internet, parking-spots, and all the one-time costs (such as basic furnishings) that on-campus housing usually provides.

8. Once you've lived in residence for a year or two, you may want to try your hand at being a residence adviser. The standard deal for most residences is that every floor or two needs someone to show the new students the ropes and generally keep order. In return for taking on this gargantuan task, you usually get free room and board, not to mention a few other perks. In addition to the large monetary incentive, your having been a residence adviser looks great on your résumé.

Random General Tips for Student Living

Regardless of where you choose to live, here are some random tips that might save you some major time and headaches while you're in school.

1. Whether you are moving in to a place on campus or off campus, filling out a prior-damage report soon after you move in is a must. Residences require you to do this anyway, for their legal protection and yours. Some unscrupulous landlords, on the other hand, might try to skip that step, in the hope that they can charge you for any prior damage when you move out. There are many places in life where you can cut corners and get away with being lazy—this isn't one of them. Make the report as detailed as you can, and do it right away. Then make copies, and keep them for yourself. If you're with a landlord, get him to sign the report, and get copies that include his signature. This legal document could save you a lot of money down the road.

2. Even if you and your science-lab partner are "BFFs", you still need to iron out a few details before moving in together. We

have seen several really good friends have their relationships severely strained by trying to live under the same roof. Try to agree on some ground rules before Day One, even if this makes you seem slightly OCD and a little bossy. Believe us when we say it's a small price to pay for preventing major conflicts down the road. Also, make sure that everyone's name is on the lease: if one roommate is liable and two others aren't, guess who will care a whole lot more when the party gets a little crazy. For a list of topics that potential roommates might want to discuss, check out this article on Justin's website for more information: *MyUniversityMoney.com/living-with-roommates-part-1.*

3. There are so many tips for saving money on groceries and utilities that they could make up a book all by themselves. We definitely recommend looking into this, and we have several tips on Justin's websites in case you're interested. Check out *YoungandThrifty.ca* in addition to the aforementioned *MyUniversityMoney.com.*

4. If you're having a hard time finding a decent place to rent (a major concern on many campuses), then harness the power of your network. Get on Facebook and use it for something other than posting generic pictures of yourself at the beach. Students often recommend new tenants to the landlord to take their place when they leave. As long as the incoming tenants have had a good record as renters, the landlord probably will be grateful for the low-maintenance referral. What about your friend's aunt, whose bridge partner is a property manager? Let her know you're a low-risk renter and have been in the market for a while. It should go without saying that you should add *Kijiji.ca* to your web browser's Bookmarks or Favourites bar and get a jump on properties right away.

5. Decide early which option is best for you and then get the paperwork done yesterday. Whether you are looking at housing on campus or off, the earlier you make sure the details are in

place, the less stress you will put on yourself. Scraping the bottom of the barrel and sitting on waiting lists for places that are forty-five minutes from your campus is not a good start to your school year.

6. Never let the beer fridge go empty.

BUYING YOUR OWN PLACE

One interesting option several families have pursued to their benefit is to buy a house close to campus and then have the children pay rent to their parents to cover the mortgage. When this plan works well, the student usually has a few friends as roommates who can be trusted to pay rent on time and not destroy the house (or at least help fix it when they do). This option makes even more sense for parents who have more than one child attending post-secondary studies in the same general area.

Because the average student will spend about $30,000 in rent or residence fees while earning a degree (and that's a conservative estimate), there is a strong argument for paying that money to your parents and building equity in a house. (Equity is the part of a house that your parents do not owe any money on. As they pay down the mortgage loan they used to buy the house, they're said to be building equity.) Let's check out the math for a hypothetical family with three children attending school in the same town. If they buy a four-bedroom house for $300,000 and spread the mortgage payments over twenty-five years (with a standard 20-percent down payment), and if they get a 3.9-percent interest rate to guarantee low costs for the long term, the monthly mortgage payment will be about $1,250. Most students pay $400 to $600 every month to live close to campus. If you charge the minimum of that range and get a rent-paying occupant for each of the four bedrooms (the three siblings and a roommate), you have $1,600 in cash coming in every month to offset the $1,250 mortgage bill. Add in repairs, property tax, and all that other fun stuff, and you might not make a whole lot of money overall—but you are building some pretty substantial equity, instead of forking over money to another property owner (whether it is a university residence or an apartment landlord).

Some people will quickly point out that you have to claim the rental money as income and that you have to pay taxes on it. While that is true, remember to factor in tax deductions for mortgage interest, property taxes, insurance, and upkeep on a rental property. To top it all off, you parents can actually pay your child a salary to be the "property manager" and that is also tax-deductible.

Here are some points to consider when you're thinking about investing in a house or condo for your children to live in while they attend school:

1. You might read national headlines saying certain real-estate markets are bubbles right now, but in our experience the housing value close to major campuses never really goes down too much. Location, location, location, right?

2. On the other hand, real-estate investment is never a sure thing, and many financial professionals in Canada are advising most people to stay away from it—especially in major urban markets.

3. Vacancy rates anywhere near most of the major campuses across Canada at the time of writing are extremely low and have been for some time. Buying property allows you to be on the profitable side of that supply-and-demand curve. Your children won't have to pay increasing rents, and at the same time you will be able to charge higher levels of rent to everyone else.

4. Your children will never have to worry about where they will live next school year and the hassle of moving. They also won't have to deal with a residence adviser they don't like, or a jerk of a landlord (well . . . at least we hope they won't consider their landlord a jerk). That stability is worth something and makes it easier for

them to do their best in school.

5. When your son or daughter graduates, he or she can buy the house from you at a discount and start building his or her own credit rating with a house that's in a desirable location. Your child can even begin renting out to the next generation of students to supplement his or her income.

6. Living in their own place and being their own "property manager" forces your kids to learn basic home-maintenance and handyman skills—which sure beats paying $100-an-hour contractors.

7. When you're a landlord, there is always a risk posed by your tenants. While your kids' friends may be fun to party with, the question of whether they should live together and you should trust them in a business sense can be a whole other matter. It probably wouldn't be a bad idea to get a basic rental contract from a lawyer, just so everyone's on the same page from Day One.

8. If you intend to sell the rental property when the kids have finished school, keep in mind that any capital gains you made on what you paid for the house are taxable (unlike any capital gains on your principal residence). The silver lining if the local real-estate market takes a dip and you sell at a loss is that you can use that loss to offset other investment income at tax time.

SUBLETTING

When summer rolls around, many students leave their fall and winter homes to pursue work, head back home to live with their parents, or both. If you are renting an apartment these days and are able to negotiate an eight-month contract, then kudos to you: most landlords work only in twelve-month contracts. This inevitably means your apartment will be sitting there for four months unoccupied while you are still paying rent on it. One way to reduce the blow to your wallet in this scenario is to look into subletting your rental for the period when you'll be gone. When you sublet, someone rents your apartment or room from you while you're away. It can be a great way to put some cash in your pocket over the summer. Most landlords are understanding when it comes to subletting, and some even have waiting lists that make the process very easy. Still, before going further, you should investigate the laws about subletting in your province, and you should look at that contract you signed last year to see what it says about subletting.

If you choose to sublet, you should consider that there is often a glut of student rentals that go on the market in May. To increase your chances of finding a good subletting tenant quickly, here are some things you can do. First, get on top of things early. The sooner you get the word out among your friends and contacts, the better. Printing a few homemade advertisements to post in high-traffic areas and making a *Kijiji.ca* advertisement aren't bad ideas either. Also, consider giving a discount of ten to twenty percent on the rent you pay, in order to stand out a little. Because there is so much competition, you might have to advertise a lower price to get noticed. Besides, even though that discount will come out of your pocket, having someone else pay eighty or ninety percent of your rent for you is better than zero percent, right? The sooner you get the sublet contract signed (often your landlord will have a template with blanks to fill in), the easier your life will be. Some people think nothing of blowing off an appointment to view the apartment, and the whole process can quickly become a time black hole. Because of this drain on effort, and because of the advantages to be gained by hitting the market first, the sooner you start the better.

While there is often wording in subletting contracts to give you some protection from people who sublet from you, it is still much easier to deal with good tenants. If you can find people you know and trust to sublet from you for the summer, do everything you can (including offering discounts) to persuade them to choose your offer. Jerks who trash the place or don't want to work with you can make your life miserable and cause more headaches than they're worth.

FURNISHING

Please, please, don't be one of those guys or gals who spend their student-loan cheques on new couches and "sweet" entertainment setups. That is the epitome of dumb debt. Do you really need new stuff that stands a pretty decent chance of getting wrecked anyway? Do you want to be worried about your precious suede furniture every time you invite your buddies over? Besides, it is a hallowed student tradition to beg, borrow, and "steal" furniture as creatively as possible.

In our opinion, you should take pride in amassing the motliest set of furnishings, with the greatest collection of stories possible. For example, when we were in school, Kyle's significant other, Molly, had a buddy who worked for a private agency that picked up large items that people no longer wanted but didn't have the means or motivation to move themselves. One day, he called her and said that he had a matching couch and loveseat that he was removing from an elderly woman's house; he said they weren't exactly "ballin'" but were in pretty good shape. After Molly accepted, he simply dropped the couches off on her lawn that day, and they were perfectly fine. She used the furniture for a couple years; then it ended up in the house Kyle was renting with a couple of friends for a while; and finally the happy couple took the set with them when they started working, because they still didn't have a ton of money with which to splurge on new furniture. The best part was that if anyone ever spilt drinks or macaroni and cheese on the couches, it was no big deal, because the total investment in the couches didn't exactly break the bank.

Check with family and friends. You might be able to sweet-talk your uncle and aunt into letting you have that "retro" couch in their basement if you come and pick it up. Many students we know inherited stuff from all over. Who really cares whether it matches anyway, as long as it serves its purpose at this point in your life? Beggars can't be choosers. If you absolutely must spend money, or you crave a little selection, then check out the local buy-and-sells or go on Kijiji. Finally, second-hand places, such as Value Village, are a great place to pick up desks, shelves, and the like, in case you need something for your room.

Chapter 2 Summary

- The easiest way to save money while going to school is to live at home!
- Living on campus means meeting new people, no cooking or dishes, no wasted commuting time, and round-the-clock access to campus services.
- Living on campus means eating cafeteria food and constant access to tempting distractions.
- Living on campus often costs more per month than living off campus. But the savings in commuting and in not being stuck paying rent on a place you don't want to occupy in the summer can quickly make up the difference.
- Buying a house or condo near campus can be a smart investment for students and their parents.
- Subletting your rented house or apartment can be a great way to save a little cash over the summer, but be sure to familiarize yourself with the details.
- You're a student—furnishing an apartment means begging, borrowing, and "stealing" anything that doesn't have bed bugs!

CHAPTER THREE

FINDING YOUR POT OF GOLD (SCHOLARSHIPS, BURSARIES, AND GRANTS)

WHAT would you say if we told you that every year in Canada about $7-million in free money earmarked just for post-secondary students went unclaimed? What if we went on to say that the $7-million in question was better than winning the lottery, because you wouldn't have to pay taxes on it? If you were a poor, starving student trying to gather the thirty-seven different pieces of information that you needed for a student-loan application, would your ears immediately perk up?

The truth is that every year across our country we set aside about $70-million for scholarships, bursaries, and grants (hereafter collectively called "scholarships" and "awards", because we're lazy) and ten percent of that goes unclaimed! Doesn't that seem a little crazy to you? We hear about all these students in the news complaining about record levels of student debt and rising tuition, and yet we collectively can't even be bothered to reach out and grab from a huge pot of gold sitting right in front of us. Scholarships are probably the most underrated aspect of personal finance for students, and they can make your life a whole lot easier.

How much can you realistically get through awards? Obviously this depends a lot on your personal background and résumé; but, if you're an average post-secondary student (not an "average" genius and not an "average" stud athlete), you can probably gain thousands of dollars in scholarships—if you apply yourself properly.

If you're in high school right now, congratulations! You still have the maximum amount of time to cash in your lottery ticket. There are so many awards waiting for you on graduation day and when you first apply to post-secondary schooling that it's like shooting fish in a barrel. You see, there are these crazy people who just want to help others reach their educational goals. They probably don't know you (yet), but they want to give you money just for trying hard at something. Economists have this saying, that there's no such thing as a free lunch; but we say scholarships come pretty close.

There are definitely chapters in this book that upon re-reading make us think "If only we had applied those strategies from Day One, we would've had a lot more money on graduation day." One of the key reasons why we were able to make so many mistakes early in our post-secondary adventures, live away from home, and still graduate debt-free was our success in the scholarship world. Earning scholarship money allows you to survive much of your financial learning-curve without a lot of stress, and it has many spinoff benefits too. The great part is that, even though we weren't standout students at the post-secondary level, we still each received thousands of dollars in awards money. Justin, by his own admission, was certainly not an "elite" student, and yet people were often throwing money at him. Kyle had solid marks, but very few of the *A*+ grades that most students believe they need to have in order to be considered for awards. In truth, he received $13,000 to $14,000 in scholarships during the five years when he was in post-secondary studies full time. Most of that was awarded on the basis of criteria other than grades (or at least in addition to them).

At the school where Kyle now teaches, one of the key points the staff drive home to grade-twelve students is that they should apply for every scholarship they can find. At first they're dubious, saying things like "I'm really busy, and I don't really have time for that stuff. Besides, don't you have to be like really smart and incredible to get scholarships?" You see, that's the beauty of this whole thing. Almost all high-school and post-secondary students (including those at Kyle's school) honestly believe this fallacy about qualifying for scholarships. The result of that thinking is that very few people see themselves as "worthy" of winning scholarships, and suddenly you have $7-million unclaimed—which you can go after!

In the past two years, the small, rural public school Kyle teaches at has produced about fifty graduates. As in any graduating class, a sizeable percentage of these students have decided to enter the workforce straight out of high school (roughly sixty percent), and many others have decided on a variety of post-secondary schooling options. Of the students who have gone on to more schooling, about fifteen have applied for a wide range of scholarships; and, in the past two years, those graduates of this tiny prairie school have been awarded about $150,000 in scholarships, bursaries, and grants before they've even set foot on a campus. Math isn't exactly our thing, but being given a cheque for an average of $10,000 before your first day of classes probably goes a long way towards helping with those student-debt figures we keep hearing about. The students who have won these awards are talented people (and admittedly two of the scholarships were each over the $20,000 mark and have thrown off the average), but they've also known how to tilt the game in their favour. Now you can too.

Even if you think you're too busy to apply for awards, we beg you to reconsider. Think about the cost–benefit ratio of applying for scholarships. How hard is it really to get out your laptop and fill in a few forms? Is a 600-word essay really going to kill you? What if you get *thousands of dollars* in return? If you think it isn't worth your time, consider the minimum-wage jobs many of you have had. If your hourly wage is $10 and you get a scholarship of $1,000 (relatively small), that scholarship is the equivalent of at least *110 hours' work* (once you factor in the deductions that come off your paycheque). Think hard about how many hours 110 really is (almost *three weeks* at full time) and how much *effort* that requires at your job.

Still think you don't have a spare hour to get a few applications together? Many teachers (including Kyle) allow students to use scholarship-application essays as substitutes for certain assignments or as extra-credit projects. Ask your teachers whether this is an option with them. Many of us nerdy, educational types will be so happy to have students who are interested in taking initiative that we'll probably agree to anything if you catch us at a weak moment.

WHERE TO FIND SCHOLARSHIPS

There's no doubt that, in today's digitally dominated world, those who know how to use technology to their benefit have a huge advantage. There are several great websites that not only list awards from all over Canada but also let you create personalized profiles that filter out many scholarships that you don't qualify for and then email specific ones right to your inbox. This is a great timesaving tool. Starting with these sites, you should get a pretty good idea of what's available:

- AUCC.ca (Association of University and Colleges of Canada)
- GlobeCampus.ca
- OnCampus.Macleans.ca
- ScholarshipsCanada.com
- SchoolFinder.com
- StudentAwards.com (Be sure to check out the great little forum.)

Once you've set up profiles on these sites, use that handy little tool called a search engine. In case you're wondering, back in B.G. times (Before Google) we just had an elaborate system of pigeons and smoke signals that sent out scholarship messages and brought in replies—and you think you have it tough! Use the Web to check out the sites for each of your parents' employers. Often these places have awards that are specifically designated for employees' children. Next, take a gander at the pages of any club, team, group, or institution that you're involved with. If you were a referee, in 4-H, a member of student council, or an athlete—if you helped coach a youth sport—if you do your banking somewhere—or if you're connected in any way to any of 101 other things, there might be a scholarship waiting for you that has very little competition for it.

If you're in high school, harass your career counsellor and teachers. Here's one of those truisms that every teacher will admit if cornered unawares but usually will never state officially: the squeaky wheel gets the grease. We teachers really wish we could say that, if you timidly ask for something once and then never follow up, you'll be rewarded one hundred percent of the time for being respectful and humble. The truth is that your request probably will be buried under an avalanche of other time demands. What you have to say is important—so keep saying it! Keep asking for help, and keep asking people whether they're aware of any new awards or scholarships available. In the world of edu-speak, we call this "advocating for yourself". Kyle's mom just called it "Not taking 'No' for an answer!"

If you're already in post-secondary studies, stop by your Financial Aid and Awards office and Student Union office. One of the neatest tricks we picked up in university is to make friends with people in the Financial Aid and Awards office. Students who were friends with people in that office often got some very advantageous phone calls. Remember all those awards that go unclaimed because they don't have any applicants? There were many occasions when Financial Aid staff made discreet phone calls to friends to let them know that there was a week left until the deadline for a certain award and that they really should apply for it. When you go after for a lot of awards that have little to no competition, good things happen! New opportunities pop up in those places every day, and in many schools there are so many awards that a substantial number don't even get publicized. If you show up to your Student Union office or the Financial

Aid and Awards office and things are being run by student employees who are in over their heads and maybe a little disorganized, just smile and be patient. Showing a little empathy can take you a long way in life. Ever talked to the people who serve you your food when you go out to eat? Something for you to chew on anyway . . . (which, incidentally, is also what they say as you bite down on the new "special of the day" after being a jerk . . .).

Finally, though this might sound unlikely, just keep your eyes open, glance at bulletin boards, and talk to people. If people know you're interested, they'll be likelier to think of you when something comes up. Applying for awards and knowing that there are plenty of people who want to help support your studies are kind of a mental habit to get into.

Here's a specific guide to persuading people to give you a pot of scholarship gold.

12 Scholarship Tips Anyone Can Use

1. Quantity Is Key

> *"You miss 100 percent of the shots you never take."*
>
> —Wayne Gretzky

> *"I've failed over and over and over again in my life. And that is why I succeed."*
>
> —Michael Jordan

As you can tell, sports analogies are kind of our thing. Both Gretzky and Jordan were obviously hard workers who weren't afraid to fail. We often hear students in their second and third years of post-secondary study say things like "Scholarships are a waste of time. I applied for like three of them and like didn't even get any." Well, first of all, one of the reasons why you didn't receive any money is that you talk like someone raised in the 21st century, and the people awarding the cash you want were raised in the 20th century—so get someone "old" to look over your stuff. Seriously, though, if you apply for only the first three scholarships you find in your Google results, your chances aren't going to be very good: the top results are almost certainly very popular and have many applicants competing against you. The people who really succeed in the realm of scholarships are those who apply EVERYWHERE.

There's an ultra-successful guy out there, named Ramit Sethi, who may very well be the third coolest personal-finance author on the planet. He has his own blog and a best-selling book, called *I Will Teach You to Be Rich*. Why should you care about this dude you've never met? Because, before he got rich and told everyone else how to do it, Ramit came up with a fairly ingenious system for applying for scholarships—and earned *over $100,000* by putting a few weeks of his time into scholarship applications. He also got a huge award just for writing about how sweet Chris Rock is—honestly, this happened. Anyway, this very intelligent (and passably charismatic) guy came up with a fairly basic system that shows just how easy the scholarship process is after you do a few of them. The vast majority of scholarship applications are very similar. If you make liberal use of the relatively new inventions of the "save" button and "copy/paste" function, combined with a little creative tweaking, you can pound out dozens of applications in a short time. The more of them you do, the easier they get and the better you get at them.

We cannot overemphasize how important it is to spread your reach as far as it will go. Why aim to get *a* scholarship? Aim to get eleven of them—or more!

2. You Deserve It (at Least as Much as the Next Person)

Say it with us: "I . . . deserve . . . free . . . money." We know it would be more appropriate to say "My educational pursuits are worth supporting", but somehow it just isn't as motivational. Likely the biggest thing stopping you from raking in easy dough is your own procrastination (the student special) and your disbelief that you could be the one accepting a sweet cheque one day. This thinking usually leads students to throw half-finished applications in the recycling bin or conveniently put them on the back burner until the deadline has passed (that way you don't actually have to admit failure). Don't talk yourself out of ambition, and don't procrastinate. Just get it done.

3. Building Creative Salesmanship . . .

Put yourself in the shoes of the average person who's reviewing scholarship applications. You have dozens of responses and essays to look over, and probably either you're volunteering to do this or it's been tacked on to all your other daily administrative duties. Are you going to pay a ton of attention to every candidate?

The truth is that you, the applicant, have to do your best to make yourself stand out. We will never advocate lying or making something up, but subtle word choices are often the difference between a second look and the paper shredder. For example, which applicant would you give an award to—someone who wrote "I worked at McDonalds for two years" or the person who states "I built my practical business and communication skills in an entry-level position while learning how to contribute positively to building a team atmosphere. I learned the value of team support, clear directions, multitasking, and positive communication from a variety of perspectives, while being trusted with gradually increasing levels of responsibility at the 'McJob' I worked at for two years"? See the difference there? Same exact experience, but one person can communicate creatively. For many of us, salesmanship does not come naturally, especially when our own qualifications are the product we have to sell. The only ways to get better are to practice; to ask for constructive criticism; and to learn the techniques in such cool books as *How to Win Friends and Influence People*, by Dale Carnegie.

When in doubt, give your old teacher a call: we love to help former students achieve goals; it gives us the warm fuzzies. In case this doesn't work, there are usually résumé-building sessions offered on most post-secondary campuses; the principles are the same. If all else fails, find one or two starving successful English majors who have bleak career prospects. They'll probably do almost anything for a beverage of their choice and a massive boost to their egos.

4. ...With Specific, Concrete Examples

If you Google "scholarship tips" or "résumé tips", you'll find everyone telling you to be creative by using active verbs (as if anyone knows what those are anymore) and basically to use "flowery", creative language. Don't do this in an abstract way. If the words don't actually relate to anything or you don't know how to use them, this will just turn people off. Don't overuse such terms as "hard worker", "smart", "fast learner", "motivated", etc. We're not telling you to avoid those phrases completely—but try to tie the nice buzzwords in to specific situations. *What makes you* "team-oriented"? Maybe you picked up these skills through various athletic teams you were a part of; or maybe it was working at McDonald's, as in our example above. The best scholarships will have more than three applicants and will require you to tie in some real substance as you dress it up a little. The more you get used to describing concrete examples of your skills, knowledge, and abilities, the easier it gets.

5. Preach to the Choir

Check the application and any information advertised with the scholarship. There are often great tips on what buzzwords administrators will be seeking when they look over applications. Often these are in the "Criteria" section. Some common examples are citizenship, diversity, and leadership. Simply take the description, language, and organization you've used in other applications and tailor them to the theme of the new one. We were big fans of glorifying whatever we wanted to say by writing this: "I was able to maintain a full course load with a _____ GPA, while doing _____." Then we would simply fill in an activity that pertained to the group, club, or organization, or the theme of the scholarship. By identifying the theme and goals of the sponsor, you're giving yourself a huge advantage in how you portray yourself.

It also doesn't hurt to whip out that smartphone that you're permanently connected to and do some quick background research on the organization, individual, or institution that's sponsoring the award. Think about how an activity such as coaching youth sports could be highlighted slightly differently if you were focusing on citizenship, or diversity, or leadership. Certainly you could pull concrete examples concerning each of those motifs from your coaching experience but, without knowing where you're going, it's often tough to get there.

6. No Unforced Errors

In case you've never watched tennis (we don't either; tennis is for people who can't play real sports . . . a buddy told us about this once), an unforced error is what happens when a player screws up something that was relatively easy and it results in a point for the opposing player. A similar idea would be the plain old "error" in baseball. Unforced errors in sports might be maddening to the players making them, but they're fairly easily explained by the fact that those players have to react extremely quickly and have little time to contemplate their manoeuvres.

That excuse doesn't work for your scholarship application and the accompanying essay. It really isn't that hard to proofread once for content, once for word choice, and once for grammar. One trick Kyle picked up is to read his writing backwards. This keeps him from skimming words and having his brain subconsciously fill in what he *meant* to say. Of course, if you can track down one of those destitute English majors again, getting another pair of eyes to take a look at it for you is never a bad move.

One thing we have noticed in our workplaces is that some of us humans are not very good at following directions. We're looking at you keeners out there who routinely go over the word limits. The people who look at these applications are not your ELA teacher, and they have a lot to do (or at least they pretend they do), so you will not gain any fans by writing your memoirs.

Generally, if you can't be bothered to double-check for the little things, it's a pretty strong indicator you don't really deserve the award—and it's a great excuse for a busy person not to bother considering you.

Oh, and if you manage to miss the deadline? Doesn't it go without saying that you don't deserve the prize you're after?

7. The Vaunted Long-Term Plan

We adults have this weird fetish for planning. We love hearing that youth are tightly focused and have everything all planned out. For some reason, we'll give money to someone with an extremely specific plan before we give it to students who truthfully profess that they really have no idea what they want to do but just love learning. We're not telling anyone to *make up* long-term goals, but we're saying that if you are mulling over multiple options (and what young adult isn't?) it might be beneficial for you to focus on depicting one that is semi-related to the award you're applying for. If you don't know what career path you want to take, at least mentioning a few solid goals can help you sound more grounded and "adult-like". Having certain goals or plans when you graduate or in your first year of post-secondary education doesn't mean you won't change your mind after all, and it doesn't mean you have to stick with them no matter what.

8. Aim for the Ones That You're Too Busy For

If you look at an award and think to yourself, "Man, that's too much work. Maybe I should skip it"—then do that one! It's pretty basic logic: the more work something is to apply for, the less competition you'll have.

Don't assume you aren't good enough for it, either. The top students often get automatic huge scholarships to go to post-secondary institutions, and many of them will go to schools in the United States—both of which leave more great options available to people who think they aren't "good enough".

Persistence and quantity will be rewarded. Ever wonder how China climbed to the top of the gold medal count at the Summer Olympics? You rarely see Chinese athletes in the finals of the 100-metre dashes or basketball (although admittedly they've dominated gymnastics over the past few Olympiads). You see, China makes a concerted effort to allow everyone else to compete in the "showcase sports" and focuses much of its attention on the trampoline and synchronized diving. This is a very effective way to pile up medals, and the same strategy can be applied to lesser-known scholarships that are too difficult to have much competition for.

9. Get the Right People in Your Corner

When you're asking people to be your references, it's important to think about what they will say about you. We constantly watch as applicants choose individuals who may be good people and have favourable opinions of the applicants, but who don't actually know much about them or are not good communicators in the medium chosen for the recommendation (whether phone call, email, or letter). That's not what you want. Remember, the idea here is to get someone to sing your praises and make you stand out.

One other suggestion is to take the notes you made when you began applying for scholarships—the notes of all your extracurricular activities, achievements, volunteering experience, academic excellence, etc.—and make copies of them for your references. Often, your references are busy people and they can forget certain things or give an incomplete picture of what you've accomplished. Giving them copies of your notes will save them time (which they'll love you for), and it will ensure a top-notch recommendation.

Finally, we've each even offered to write our own "rough draft" of a recommendation if the person one of us wanted as a reference was too busy to give it careful consideration. What usually happens in that situation is that you write a draft, give it to your reference, and let him or her make any preferred changes to it before signing off (and people rarely will make changes if you do it right). While this might seem presumptuous or somehow dishonest, we believe it's a fairly widespread practice and, just as long as you're not making references up or signing people's names without their permission, we do not believe it's dishonest. This gives you the chance to craft a decisive picture of yourself for whoever is administering the award.

10. Momentum and Stepping-Stones

The interesting way this whole awards thing works is that being recognized once makes it easier to be recognized again—and even easier the third time. For better or for worse, we live in a credential-obsessed society. This means that if the people administering the scholarships can look down and see that someone else thought you were legitimate (as proven by your shiny scholarship) then they too can safely think highly of you. This is similar to what psychologists call the "halo effect" (which is worth looking up). You thus can quickly gain momentum by applying for numerous scholarships and using those successes as launch pads for your next round of applications.

Of course, when you earn a scholarship, the money is not the only reward you receive: the connections network that many award winners gain can be more beneficial than the additions to their bank accounts. Similarly, awards give you solid proof of how great you are, which you can throw on résumés and mention in job interviews.

11. Honesty Really Is the Best Policy

While this would seem to be fairly common sense, it still is often forgotten. If you're found to have lied on your scholarship applications, not only can you lose your cash award, but also you can actually face academic penalties and a permanent mark on your transcript. Already spent the money? You'll still have to pay it back.

We know it can be tempting to invent extracurricular activities to make yourself appear well rounded, or to erase "in the top five percent" and replace it with "in the top one percent" in order to seem more elite; but just resist that urge. There are plenty of awards to go around, and a reputation for dishonesty will keep you from getting any of them.

12. Watch Out for the Scam Artists

Sadly, there are scuzzy individuals out there who take advantage of young people looking for support for their education. Here's the general rule: if they ask you for money, a credit- or debit-card number, or large amounts of personal-identification information, you probably should steer clear! If you have any questions about this, be sure to check with your career counsellor or student adviser before applying.

Chapter 3 Summary

- $7-million in scholarship money goes unclaimed every year in Canada. Is some of it yours?
- Scholarships, bursaries, and grants are non-taxed lotteries that only students get to enter.
- There are scholarships for every type of person.
- There is no such thing as applying for too many scholarships.
- Scholarships can be found online, at school, through your place of work, and in dozens of other places. Keep your eyes open.
- Use our tips to give yourself a massive advantage over the competition.

CHAPTER FOUR

PARTY LIKE A ~~ROCKSTAR~~ STUDENT

AT the risk of sounding like the 1,001 other student guides on the market, and despite the title of our book, we actually don't recommend spending your entire student loan on a week of booze-driven hedonistic fantasyland. Partying and alcohol are not cheap, to say the least; and we saw some of our friends develop major problems from consistent overconsumption of alcohol. But both of us will be right up front with you: we spent a ton of money at our campus bar. If we had taken the money that we "invested" in our favourite brews on campus and had put it in an RRSP, it probably would be about $150,000 by the time we were sixty-five.

One of our friends in university resolved that he wasn't going to drink. Instead, he used the money he would've spent on booze to buy a big-screen TV and several other cool toys that we all were jealous of. On top of that, he'd often hang out with us and drink nothing harder than Pepsi. So, believe it or not, you don't actually need alcohol to have a good time.

That said, if we could do it over again we probably wouldn't change a thing. There is a certain paradox to writing a personal-finance guide about being responsible with money and then readily admitting that you like the taste of beer—a lot. When you really break it down, alcohol and other expenses commonly associated with young-adult partying are completely a luxury that you don't really need. In fact, it's a luxury that not only costs money up front but also limits your productivity overall.

So how do we satisfy both sides of ourselves? How do we semi-responsibly build for the future, yet enjoy being young because we only live once?

Like many things in life, it's about balance and management. No one wants to be thinking about affording things next week when there are a great concert and after-party to go to tonight. If you want to get the full mileage out of your meagre student bankroll, however, making a few of these choices is a necessity. If you succumb to the cliché of "keeping up with the Joneses" and try to get respect and validation by spending money, a financial disaster is somewhat inevitable. Whether we're talking about looking trendy with the latest $6 brew or with a new pair of $100+ jeans, trying to build a reputation or an image around spending money just isn't sustainable for the vast majority of students. Prioritizing exactly what concerts or sporting events we most want to see, or where we want to spend our clothing dollars, is a concept that's difficult for most us, especially because we're part of the "I want what I want, and I want it now" generation.

Anyway, because the title of this book promises some hops-and-barley-driven content, here's the best advice we have for beer-loving post-secondary students: as the legendary Forrest Griffin once said, "Beer is an acquired taste, so you might as well acquire a taste for cheap beer." (In case you're keeping track, we just broke the records for both the number of professional-cage-fighter quotes and the number of beer quotes in a personal-finance book.) While our Pepsi-downing friend never allowed sudsy goodness to pass between his lips, this isn't the norm in our experience. That being said, one quick way to ensure that you add insult to your morning injury (hangover) is to wake up to an empty wallet from trying to impress everyone by buying drinks for the crowd. Men seem to be especially vulnerable to this temptation if they happen to be trying to impress a pretty girl and her friends. We're not saying it never happened to us, gentlemen, but we can honestly tell you that the low success rate probably doesn't justify the investment for most of us.

Studies show that the modern Canadian student who partakes of the traditional frosty-beverage form of student entertainment consumes thirteen drinks in an average week—almost two a day. It doesn't take advanced calculus to figure out that paying double or triple the price per drink by going to bars is not making the most efficient use of your booze-to-dollars ratio. If you do most of your drinking with your crew before heading out for the night (other than your designated driver, of course), you'll save yourself some serious dough in the long run. It has been scientifically proven that ten millilitres of hard alcohol are all that's needed to maintain your level of inebriation (a.k.a. "buzz") no matter how large a person you are. Do what you will with that information. (How much fun was that study to be a part of?)

Here are a few more quick tips to save you money when you hit up the clubs and pubs:

1. If you work in the service industry (as many students do), keep an eye open for "industry nights", where showing a pay stub from your workplace can get you free admission and a few other perks. In our experience, employees in the service sector generally have each other's backs when it comes to this sort of thing.

2. Call a few of the top spots in your city to see who offers the best birthday deal. Playing the top promotions against each other often will get you and twenty of your friends in the door "VIP" (skipping the lines, etc).

3. Become friends with the bartenders and staff at your usual hangout. You know the place . . . the one "where everybody knows your name." For us it was our campus pub. If you're a regular and you treat the staff well, they will remember it when it comes

time to determine the priority for drink orders and other little perks.

4. Ditto making friends with the bouncers. There is a reason why some people get to go the front of the line and slip past everyone else as they give a unique handshake to the bros with bulging biceps. That reason is that they treat the big guys nicely and maybe buy them the odd drink after their shifts are done. Also, if any tough guys or gals try to pick a fight with you, guess who your good friend the bouncer is going to kick out.

5. If you're into student government, or are responsible for planning any events that include alcohol, it doesn't hurt to become friends with the liquor or beer reps. Often, in exchange for long-term loyalty, personal discounts and freebies can be plentiful.

6. Bartenders are often so busy that they don't even notice who is tipping them or how much the tip is. If your goal is to encourage better service by throwing money at people, it is much more beneficial to direct your patronage to a single bartender at each place you frequent. When you consistently treat "your" bartenders right, they probably will reciprocate with generous portion sizes and the odd "on-the-house special" if they're any good at what they do.

7. Some people recommend putting a credit card down at the beginning of the night and using a tab so that you can tip your usual percentage at the end of the night, as opposed to saying, "Keep the change", after every purchase and inadvertently tipping a huge percentage. This is a solid approach in theory, but credit-card tabs and alcohol are often an unholy mix. Make sure you're comfortable with the bar scene before attempting to execute this tip.

Speaking of being a bar star: drinks are often only the beginning of your costs for a night on the town. Again, we don't mean to get up on a soapbox here and guilt-trip anyone into making different lifestyle choices. We're simply stating the reality of the fact that when most young people hit the bar scene they forget to budget for tips on drinks, cab rides, and late-night snack stops, among other things. Lowering your inhibitions doesn't just affect your choice in kissing-partners: it also means that trips to the ATM get easier as the night goes on.

If you're really looking to limit your spending for a certain period, one way to gain some serious favour from your friends is to volunteer to be the designated driver for the night. We should reiterate here that drunk driving (or "mildly buzzed" driving) is not cool under any circumstances. From a purely financial perspective, volunteering to be DD will usually get you free soft drinks all night if you ask one of the bartenders, or give you an excuse to have a quiet recovery night at the hipster coffee shop around the corner while you wait for your buddies. On a more practical note, don't be that person who promises to be the DD and then ends up having "just a few". Drunk driving kills thousands of people every year in North America (it works out to more than one every hour), and it would have been very easy to let every one of those people keep on enjoying life. On a less moral (and less important) note, driving drunk is a serious offence in Canada. It carries large fines and a licence suspension, and could greatly harm your ability to find or keep a job. Needless to say, in addition to all the other problems associated with drunk driving, it could also cost you a great deal of money.

Justin has experimented heavily with making several types of alcohol. If you want to try a new hobby and severely cut down on your booze costs, all while creating a huge demand for your friendship, he definitely recommends trying your hand at homemade beer or wine. It's really not that hard with the specialized kits they make these days. While it isn't legal to sell the booze you make, it's entirely acceptable to have everyone owe you favours in exchange for the odd gift of a bottle of wine or a pint of your latest pale ale. If some of your early creations aren't quite up to retail standards, don't sweat it: in our experience, they all taste the same after the first dozen anyway.

The hidden costs of splurging on entertainment (specifically the frosty-beverage kind) include withdrawing from courses and therefore having to spend another year of your life on school. These costs can really get to you. Another year of school is another year you're not earning the paycheque you want. Plus, you have to pay for those courses all over again, in addition to another year of living expenses. Kyle was fortunate enough as a young student to read a column that stated that the average university course comprised twenty-eight to forty individual classes. At around $600 in tuition per course, you burn roughly $20 every time you skip a class because you're hung over. A few final expenses that can accompany those "legendary" nights out are lost possessions (smartphones, anyone?), damage to your property, and fines for what you did when your inhibitions had melted away. Make no mistake: while beer tastes great, it can be a very expensive sport/pastime/semi-religion if you decide to use it extensively.

SMOKING AND DRUGS

Even though we get paid to give advice to young adults, we still don't feel entirely comfortable getting up on a soapbox and telling people what practices they should consider moral or immoral. We liked to consume copious amounts of beer at one point in our lives (sadly, these days it is decisively less), and many people wouldn't consider that a good choice as far as our physical and mental health were concerned. That being said, if you choose to make cigarettes or drugs a part of your life, your financial climb just got a lot steeper, in addition to the obvious lifestyle challenges you're choosing to take on. If you are a half-a-pack-a-day smoker, you're allowing $2,184 a year to go up in smoke (assuming it costs an average of $12 for a pack of cigarettes). Beyond all the long-term health costs that probably will hit you later in life, you are basically throwing away the equivalent of a week-long luxury trip to Cancun, Banff, or Vegas every year, just for the sake of your daily nicotine fix.

When it comes to drugs, the costs are much harder to quantify and obviously vary widely with the poison you pick (one of the few times that's not just a figure of speech). Truthfully, we've seen some students who had recreational marijuana habits and who managed to do quite fine (although it cost them a fair amount of money in fast food, Slurpees, and Cheetos, in addition to the actual marijuana). There are even some convincing arguments for making cannabis legal. However, in addition to the upfront costs of the drugs you buy, you should consider the *hidden* costs, such as a drop in academic performance, consequences in your work life (random drug testing?), fines for being caught with the substance, and several other negative spin-offs that are hard to predict, including a criminal conviction. Needless to say, if your choice of drug is "harder" than the leafy variety we just discussed, the stakes become even higher, and the possibility of steep decline in your overall standard of living becomes much greater. As one of our mentors (Mr. Garrison from the acclaimed animated series *South Park*) is fond of stating, "Drugs are bad . . . mmmmmkay?" All we're saying is, before you make an adult decision about using substances like nicotine, marijuana, or "harder" stuff, just be aware of the sacrifices you are making elsewhere in life, including your physical health and financial well-being. Some people still decide it's worth it—we're not those people.

THE PARTY EXPERIENCE

To help you minimize the alcohol-fuelled destruction of your wallet, we thought we'd throw a few quick party pointers your way that'll probably come in handy at some point in your academic journey:

1. When hosting a party, buy food in bulk. That two-kilogram bag of tortilla chips will taste just as good as the fancy stuff after a

keg and a half of beer.

2. While filling half your cart with cheap food, fill the other half with large amounts of no-name cleaning-supplies. You'll thank yourself in the morning.

3. Clean everything non-essential out of the refrigerator. You'll want maximum beer-chilling capacity and, as an added benefit, it's a pretty well established custom that the house keeps any alcohol overages to offset expenses. On the flip side, when you attend someone else's party, leaving the last couple of cold ones or shots is expected, and being the ultra-cheapo who takes the last two back home is not cool.

4. Party-proof your crib. Place all remotes, speakers, monitors, etc., out of harm's way. You don't want to be left holding the bill when Mr. "Dude, It's Not My Fault, I Was Drunk" stumbles into the new TV you got for Christmas.

5. When you buy a keg, the house always drinks for free. Pay your football buddy (or a capable stand-in) to collect the $10 and be the beer custodian for the evening. It will save you time and effort later.

ACTIVITIES YOUR LIVER WILL THANK YOU FOR

Rather than bore you with endless philosophical theories about saving money or more tips on how to afford copious amounts of liquid courage, we now present a handful of more-wholesome ways we've stretched our entertainment budgets over the years as students:

1. Discount night at the "cheap seats", or second-run movie theatres. Bring your own snacks for even more savings; we know it sounds cheap (O.K., it *is* cheap), but this is where many theatres make most of their money, because of the insane mark-ups

on theatre food.

2. Go check out your school's sports teams! We can't get over how few students routinely go to support their schools' sports programs right across Canada. Tickets and season passes are always dirt cheap (if not free) for students, and if nothing else it's always fun to heckle the opposing team. While the level of play is obviously slightly lower than that of professional sports, your quality of seating will more than make up the difference. Also, keep your eyes open for high-level sports events taking place at your campus facilities. At the University of Manitoba, we could routinely check out international volleyball games for peanuts.

3. If professional sports are your thing, compare options for top-notch minor-league games to the package that the professional team in town offers for a much higher price. With all the technology available today, pro sports are better viewed from your couch, in our opinion, anyway!

4. There are usually some great gigs to check out in the very inexpensive underground music world. In addition, keep your eyes peeled for free "open mic" nights, where there are some surprisingly good, and some hilariously bad, performers.

5. Join an intramural team or a student group. There's a huge variety of clubs and teams available for any taste and schedule.

6. Volunteering! We know people think of a rough-and-tumble soup kitchen when they hear the term *volunteering*, but the truth is that there are volunteers needed all over your community. If you're looking for a quick route to scholarships, this is it. In addition to being fun and giving you cool people to interact with, volunteering really does give you that warm, mushy feeling inside—which almost takes away the guilt for last Friday night.

7. If you live in residence, cheap entertainment is plentiful. Simply walk down the hall and see what people are up to!

8. Invite your buddies over for a *Rocky*-themed marathon. Drink every time you hear "Adrian" or when Paully does something inappropriate. Feel free to sub in *Star Wars*, *Mad Men*, or any other show you can lose yourself in for a lazy day.

9. Coupons aren't really our thing, but there are definitely savings to be had if you crack open that coupon book your aunt bought you. Also check out *Groupon.com*, *LivingSocial.com*, and similar sites for even more savings.

10. Museums. O.K., so we know the word *geek* just flashed through your head half a dozen times, but what about the local sports hall of fame or a cool wildlife exhibit? Most museums offer student discounts and can be pretty interesting—at least if you're not afraid to embrace your inner geek!

11. Use the Web to look up some inexpensive date ideas in your city. Rather than our giving you some generic suggestions, chances are someone in your city has generated a unique list, specific to your area, that's just waiting to be explored.

12. Keep track of dining-out specials. We always knew which night was "cheap beer and wings" night everywhere in the city. *But* don't skimp on the tip: if you can't afford to tip, you can't afford to go out to eat (especially if you'll be going back—Kyle's significant other was a waitress, so trust us on this one). You don't have to pretend to be a high-roller, but unless the service was terrible the tip is more or less required.

13. Board games, anyone? If you aren't secure enough to embrace your inner nerdiness without a little social lubricant, turn your high-stakes game of Risk or Monopoly into a drinking-game with your homemade or cheap beer. Landed on Boardwalk? Bottoms up!

14. While trying to be like the next poker stud on TV, don't attempt to double the money from your student loan by betting online

or at the local casino. Instead, set up a $2-to-$5 buy-in poker tournament with your pals. You can still trash-talk and feel like a hotshot—without that soul-sucking vacuumesque feeling you can get after losing a day's wages on a single hand.

15. Campus theatre productions are always cheap and can be of surprisingly high quality. Supporting your local thespians is a worthy cause in and of itself.

16. Play to your strengths as a student with a ton of flexible time by getting the mid-week bargains on entertainment. That's when demand is lower. Then, choose a cheaper option on Friday and Saturday nights, when those working stiffs take over the scene anyway.

Chapter 4 Summary

- A great way to save money is to never drink alcohol or attend parties.
- We highly recommend drinking alcohol (semi-responsibly) and attending parties.
- Partying like a student means figuring out a balance that works for you.
- Partying hard doesn't have to mean partying expensive.
- Skipping classes = flushing money down the toilet.
- You need to give your body and bank account the odd day to recover. When you do, there are tons of ways to have fun without breaking the piggy bank.

CHAPTER FIVE

GOTTA GET AWAY (STUDENT TRAVEL)

LET'S be brutally honest. For most of us who really want to keep to a strict student budget in order to minimize debt when we leave school, travel probably isn't in the cards—or at least not the airplane-dependent version. In our experience, students tend to be lured into expensive vacations through clever promotions that advertise very low prices for travel and accommodations. Usually these ads fail to highlight multiple fees, and students who don't have much experience travelling on their own are extremely vulnerable to excess spending throughout their vacations. It's simply too easy to justify binge-spending on student vacations by saying, "You Only Live Once (YOLO)! I'll never be back in _____ again!" And that's how your mom got that tattoo she doesn't like to talk about, by the way. Too many students have had a great spring break (at least as far as they can recall), only to come home to a massive Visa bill just as they should be focusing on the final stretch of the academic calendar.

We should admit up front that we certainly don't consider ourselves experts on travel. There are entire books written on the subject, and we definitely recommend a quick *Amazon.ca* search if you're serious about travelling as a student. We do know that doing a little research before you leave home can really benefit both your overall experience and your wallet. Check online before you leave to find reviews and prices for entertainment and restaurants at your destination. We're fairly convinced that, if you use the World Wide Web as the great equalizer, being your own travel agent is the best way to go. For the few trips that we have been on, planning everything has actually been a lot of fun. Such tools as *Expedia.ca*, *Kayak.com*, and *Travelocity.ca* can help you find packages to stretch that modest budget as far as it will go, and many places offer discounts for online booking. As a teacher, Kyle feels compelled to point out that this is yet another case in which it really pays to do your homework ahead of time. (And, yes, that sound you hear is his former students gagging in the background.) Here are twelve random tips that can save you some cash as you look forward to your big Spring Break adventure:

1. There are some fantastic deals available if you do your travelling outside of the normal vacation times. Tourism is just like any other business: if you travel when demand is highest, you'll definitely pay a large premium.

2. If you're not picky about where you want to go, and you love to fly by the seat of your pants, you can have great adventures just by showing up at a large airport and letting a few major airlines know that you just want to go somewhere warm. This might sound crazy, but airlines routinely offer huge last-minute discounts to fill the last few seats on planes. To the airlines, the pilot's salary and the other flying expenses are already sunk costs, so any money they get for open seats is a bonus. As long as you're flexible about times and locations, you'll probably get an offer you can't refuse.

3. For the slightly less adventurous crowd that still wants to cash in on last-minute deals, we recommend checking out the latest offerings at *RedTag.ca*. There are constantly new deals popping up if you keep your eyes open.

4. Who needs the hassle of airports and the awkwardness of a for-

eign country, anyway? We live in the greatest tourism destination for natural beauty in the entire world! Take a road trip out to the Rockies, or hike the Cabot Trail, for some cheap Canadian goodness.

5. Wherever you end up, one thing almost always stays the same: tourists pay more. Follow the locals (or bribe them) to their favourite locales and enjoy better food for a lower price. Think about it: who knows your backyard better than you do, right?

6. One major expense often overlooked by many young travellers is the cost of eating out every day. To cut down on this line of your budget, consider going to a supermarket whenever possible and then having breakfast in your room and packing lunch for the day. This still leaves supper as a chance to sample the local cuisine. Another option that some travel-savvy people prefer is to chow down on restaurant fare at lunch (prices often are lower then than at dinner) and then pack a light supper for the evening sight-seeing.

7. Stay away from tourist gift shops. Roughly ninety-eight percent of the stuff there is lame anyway, and we guarantee that one block back from the main drag of whatever town you're in you could get three of those cheesy shirts for $5 instead of $29.99 each.

8. If you're heading out of town with a group, remember to ask for group pricing ahead of time. Whether it's hotels or tours, you can almost always negotiate a group rate, because you're bringing in several customers at once.

9. Students and hostels are perfect for one another—just ask horror-movie writers. There's such a huge range of accommodations that fit under the catch-all heading "hostel" that it's difficult to generalize. Our advice is to get on that Interweb thing the kids are talking about these days and check out a few hos-

tel reviews for the places you're headed to. A good track record and cheap prices can mean serious value for you. Register with Hostelling International, at *HIHostels.ca*, for cheap tips and extensive discounts.

10. In case hostels and hotels aren't your thing, many places have great hidden accommodation gems in the form of bed-and-breakfasts. Most of these small businesses are open to large discounts for guests who are staying for an extended vacation, and a great arrangement can often be worked out for both parties. Money saved on meals, and great local guides, are just two of the perks that go along with the traditional B&B experience.

11. Don't be afraid to barter. Canadians seem to have an aversion to aggressive negotiation, but much of the rest of the world doesn't share that reluctance. Many of us therefore pay a much higher mark-up than necessary on everything from basic foodstuffs to jewellery and souvenirs, thus permanently labelling ourselves dumb tourists just asking to get fleeced.

12. We know we're supposed to tout the Travel Cuts travel agency (owned by the Canadian Federation of Students) here, but we're not sure they've ever had the best prices when we've compared options. They do offer some great advice and definitely cater to the Canadian student experience, but we honestly believe that with a couple hours and a decent Internet connection most students can get better deals for themselves than Travel Cuts or any other agency can provide.

Finally, short vacations are all well and good; but, if you truly want to experience a new culture and do it without breaking the bank, there are some other great options. The Canadian Federation of Students has a great service, the Student Work Abroad Program (SWAP). Its goal is to exchange Canadian students with those of other countries from around the globe and even find work for them in their new surroundings. Since its inception, way back in 1975, the program has sent more than 50,000 students on "working holidays". SWAP prides itself on being a full-transition service, which can help you not only with finding a job and living accommodations, but also with such things as getting a student or travel visa to your destination country. Find out more at *SWAP.ca.* There are other exchange programs worth checking out as well—again, get on the Google machine.

Finally, one strategy we've seen firsthand work pretty well for people who want to travel the world without going broke is to teach English abroad. If you were thinking about being a teacher anyway, this is a no-brainer; but you definitely don't need an education degree to pursue this. There's a variety of educational backgrounds that'll qualify you to teach English as a foreign language, and we've heard rave reviews from several of our colleagues who have taken on this challenge. Don't limit your thinking to hotels and tourist traps!

We understand you're only young once and that many people believe the only way to experience the world is as a young, adventurous adult. Just remember that the piper must eventually be paid. If the vacations you're taking now are contributing to a bigger student debt, you really have to balance the positives and negatives. Admittedly this is easier said than done; but trust us—Paris isn't going anywhere. It will wait for you. We've noticed a recent trend among some students, for whom travelling becomes almost a socially acceptable excuse for not beginning life as an adult and looking for work, or for putting off the final push in post-secondary studies. This isn't cool, and burning student-loan money on expensive overseas trips is probably responsible for much of the skyrocketing debt you see in the news right now. Go ahead and have a great time while in school. Just be creative and look for ways to travel that don't put you too far into the red.

Chapter 5 Summary

- Sticking to a student budget might mean forgoing travelling for a few years despite the loan-fuelled trips you see others making.
- Shop around to get the most for your travel dollar.
- There are several things you can do to shrink the cost of a trip substantially.
- Consider non-traditional travel, such as student-exchange programs and the SWAP experience.

CHAPTER SIX
THE BANK OF MOM AND DAD

IF you ever want to stir up a crowd, walk into a room of Canadian parents and tell them that it is only right that parents help their kids through school. We guarantee you will get an interesting variety of responses. Some parents are absolutely adamant that their precious angels should have every opportunity in the world, and consequently they will foot the bill in order to give their future astronauts, physicists, and architects every chance imaginable. Other parents steadfastly believe that, if they keep giving their children fish, they will never learn how to set a line for themselves. Meanwhile, all the "experts" out there are preaching from different gospels, ranging from "You must have $2-million in retirement savings before you worry about your child's education" to "If you don't use the RESP program, you're guaranteeing that your children start life in a hole of debt they will never climb out of." Usually these speeches are an attempt to bully you into buying one investment product or another. But none of this changes the fact that textbooks aren't cheap and, gee, Mom and Dad, don't you want your little darling to succeed?

The truth is that, by paying taxes for years, your parents (along with all the other taxpayers) are already helping pay for your education—in fact, they're paying for most of it.

We're not going to sit here as a couple of guys with no kids of our own and say that parents categorically should, or should not, help their children financially with their post-secondary efforts. We will say that we are extremely thankful that our parents chose to help us, and we think it can be a huge boost to students while they are in school; but we also see the logic behind the tough-love approach.

This much is certain: if students are supposed to figure out a rough budget for the year, they need to have some idea of how much help they can expect from their parents. The support doesn't always have to be a blank cheque: sometimes it can be as simple as stocking up on groceries a few times during the year or purchasing a new computer as a Christmas gift.

The key point here is that most parents and children don't communicate nearly enough about how they each expect school expenses to be covered, and this often results in both parties' having radically different ideas about what parents can afford to contribute and what they intend to contribute.

THE RESP—THE RRSP'S COOL LITTLE BROTHER

The primary investment vehicle through which parents can help their children is the Registered Education Savings Plan, more commonly known as the RESP. Now you don't "buy RESPs", just as you don't "buy RRSPs", because what those acronyms stand for is actually registered savings plans. You don't buy the plan: you put investments into it. Many, many parents are extremely confused about how any sort of registered plan is used, because bank employees and investment advisers make a lot of money on this confusion. Usually, these institutions get paid by simply using financial terminology that is confusing to most people and then putting people's investments into mutual funds that generate huge profits for everyone in the financial industry. Before we explain a few of the nuts and bolts about why RESPs are such a great deal, we're going to recommend

The RESP Book, by Mike Holman. As you might expect from the title, it is the authority on the topic and it answers more or less every conceivable question you might come up with. Because your parents probably want *you* to read *this* book, get *them* to read *The RESP Book*. Even though it's probably too late for them to get much benefit out of putting money into an RESP account for you, they may want to get educated in order to help one of your younger siblings, or even their grandchildren one day (in case your parents haven't reminded you, they're not getting any younger).

The idea behind RESPs is that the government wants to encourage parents to save as much money as they can for their children's education. To give parents some incentive to do this, the government will actually put money in your RESP account just as long as the parents do, and there are very few strings attached. Generally, if the government is going to give you free money, take it and run! The money the government puts in the account is called a Canada Education Savings Grant (CESG). Here is a quick, basic summary of the program (all figures are based on 2012 rules):

1. A child can be given up to $50,000 in the form of contributions to one or more RESPs. The federal government will automatically chip in twenty percent of your contribution—within certain limits: the government will contribute up to $500 a year, up to a lifetime limit of $7,200. If, for example, you have $10,000 that you can give, it's better to split it over more than one year, because the government bonus will be bigger: if you gave the full $10,000 in one year, twenty percent of that would be $2,000, but the government's contribution that year would stop at $500, and so the total government contribution added to your $10,000 would be only $500; on the other hand, if you split the $10,000 into four and gave $2,500 in each of four years, the government would contribute its $500 upper limit in each of those four years, for a total of $2,000 on top of your $10,000 gift. These contributions can pile up until the child turns seventeen. There are

some slightly more complex contribution rules in case you want to catch up on contribution years that you've missed. For a complete description of these rules, we again direct you to *The RESP Book: The Simple Guide to Registered Education Savings Plans for Canadians*, by Mike Holman.

2. Within an RESP account, there is a wide array of investment options for parents to choose from.

3. Unlike money put into an RRSP, money put into an RESP is *not* tax-deductible. You will not get a tax refund for contributing to it.

4. When money is taken out of an RESP, only the CESG and the investment gains made inside the account are taxable, and they will be taxed as income in the hands of the student. This often results in very little tax (if any) being paid.

5. With very little paperwork, money in an RESP can be transferred between siblings, in case the primary beneficiary doesn't need the money for one reason or another.

6. If RESP money remains unused, there are options for parents to roll their contributions over to an RRSP, but the CESG and its investment gains will be forfeited.

7. It's not only parents who can contribute to RESPs, but also other relatives and anyone else (although some institutions will take cheques only from the subscriber to the account). Think about a Christmas present from Grandma and Grandpa!

8. Alberta and Quebec have provincial incentives for RESPs in addition to the federal ones.

When you take out money from your RESPs (or, to be more accurate, when your parents take it out for you), you will need proof of enrolment from your Registrar's or Administrative office. Then the institution that took care of your RESP will send your parents the money, along with a document that shows how much of the withdrawal is your parents' original money and how much of it is from the CESG and investment income. Any part of the money that's not your parents' direct contribution is considered income for you and is taxable in your hands. The cool part about this is that you probably aren't making much money, and the government has a bunch of tax breaks that you can take advantage of, so you probably won't end up paying any taxes on it at all. (See CHAPTER 9, on student tax returns.)

Hey, Mom and Dad: although we strongly recommend planning ahead if you want to give your children direct financial help while they're in post-secondary education (the benefits of the RESP program are hard to ignore), there are some other options for helping your young adult children. First of all, if you and your child can still put up with each other after eighteen years, there is no denying the financial benefits of having him or her continue to live at home while going to school. Even if you charge a little rent, it's still a heck of deal. Students will quickly begin to understand that toiletries, cleaning supplies, utilities, Internet and cable connections, food, transportation, and dozens of other little expenses are much costlier than they ever would have thought. If your eighteen-year-olds are anything like we were at that age, they have little or no idea how many small costs are associated with living away from home—especially if they choose not to live in residence, where cleaning and cooking are taken care of for them.

In case you want to lend a helping hand to your child now heading into post-secondary schooling but you haven't invested in RESPs, a no-interest loan from the Bank of Mom and Dad is another option. Many parents prefer lending their adult children money, rather than giving it to them; and those parents often are willing to sacrifice the investment returns they could get with the money somewhere else, in exchange for helping out their loved ones. Compound interest on a student line of credit (or, even worse, on a credit card) can really grow quickly and hurt students before they truly understand what is happening. If parental income is too high to qualify for student loans, this might be something worth discussing.

To all you students: Whether a fantastic home-cooked meal and a little laundry detergent when you come for the holidays are all your parents have budgeted to help you out, or whether they have a nice, fat RESP waiting to come to your rescue, we cannot emphasize enough how important it is to have a frank discussion with your parents about this. In many households across Canada, discussing money with children is still a weird taboo; but, if you want to avoid a desperate late-night plea in February for help paying a huge credit-card bill, the best way to do this is to sit down with your folks early in the game.

Oh, and guys and gals? Remember to say Thanks to old Ma and Pa once in a while. We hear it goes a long way. You do want the holiday-dinner leftovers, right?

Chapter 6 Summary

- No matter what your financial situation is, you and your parents should have a clearly communicated plan in place so that everyone is on the same page.
- Registered Education Savings Plans (RESPs) are a great tool that you and your parents should be aware of.
- Parental support can take many forms other than money.
- Don't take your parents' help for granted, and do say Thank You!

CHAPTER SEVEN

STUDENT LOANS . . . JACKPOT! (NOT REALLY)

MOST of you have probably heard the term *student loan* before, and in a few different contexts. The phrase is kind of amazing in that it means radically different things in different situations. For example, if you are eighteen and have just been told your bank-account balance now that your student loan has come in, what you're really hearing is "Round of shots on me!" If you're a thirty-year-old who is still living at home because you can't repay your student loans and pay rent at the same time, the term *student loan* might be code for "black hole" or "crushing burden".

Really, student loans have gotten a pretty bad reputation as student debt levels have climbed. They are actually a pretty good deal when you consider the big picture. So what the heck is a student loan? A student loan is what you get when the government lends you money and pays the interest on that loan for you until you've finished school. In case you weren't aware, in the "real world", when people lend you money, they expect you to give them a little extra money, on top of whatever they lent you, as payment for the service of lending you the money in the first place. It helps make up for the fact that they couldn't do anything else with their money while you were using it. This extra money you pay is called **interest**, and the amount of interest you have to pay is a chosen percentage of the amount you borrowed. This is how banks make money (well, it was before bankers watched too many Wall Street movies anyway). So, when you take out a student loan, someone has to get paid in order to bother lending you the money. The government is nice enough to step in and help you out by paying the interest on this loan until you graduate and can manage for yourself. Because paying the interest on tens of thousands of student loans every year costs a fair amount of money, the government has set some pretty specific rules about who should be able to use student loans and who has enough assets to be considered sufficiently funded without the government's help.

Canadian students who apply for student loans are actually applying for two different types of loans, whether they realize it or not. The federal student-loan program is administered by the National Student Loans Service Centre (NSLSC) and is available across Canada. Most of Canada's provinces also have student-loan programs, which usually run parallel to the NSLSC's. The general rule across Canada is that sixty percent of your student-loan money will come from the federal government, and forty percent from your provincial or territorial government. It's estimated that, since Canada began offering student loans in 1964, 4.3-million students have received almost $32-billion in student loans.

While student loans are a pretty good deal, they aren't as good as having no debt at all. If these loans are used to pay for legitimate expenses that need to be covered as you push through your post-secondary journey, then probably few people will argue that they have been used irrationally. If the loans are used to pay for a luxury trip to Banff or Mexico for spring break, however, that's another story. It is essential that you realize as a young adult that statistics are pretty clear: you are likely to live past twenty-five (despite how you feel on some Sunday mornings). You need to take into account that student loans will have to be paid back, and that if you build up enough debt it can seriously cramp your style for a very long time after you graduate. There is no guarantee that a high-paying job awaits you—and your debt *will* have to be paid back, regardless of everything else (student-loan debt can even follow you through bankruptcy!). When we were eighteen, we lived in a fantasyland where life after post-secondary education was a lifetime away, and our brilliant problem-solving strategy was "I'll cross that bridge when I come to it." Nowadays, as professionals who work with young adults every day, we can safely say that that mindset is pretty much the default. We're not claiming that you have to map out life until you hit the retirement home, but thinking about the fact that one day you might not want to live in your parents' basement or drive their family van anymore is a pretty good start.

CANADA STUDENT GRANTS

When you apply for a Canada student loan, you are also applying automatically for a Canada student grant. The financial-aid and grants system was revamped in 2009, and the new version is automatically applied to all applicants without their doing anything extra. The main difference between a Canada student loan and a Canada student grant is that grants don't need to be paid back: your government is basically *giving* you money, as long as you meet certain need-based criteria. Every year, roughly 250,000 Canadian students benefit from the grant program. The amount of financial support you're eligible to receive through the grant program depends on your family's income status as defined by the federal and provincial governments. If you qualify for a Canada Student Grant, you can receive that money without actually having to take a student loan, so it's definitely worth looking into.

To determine whether your family meets the qualifications for low-income or middle-income status, check out the chart at *canlearn.ca/eng/postsec/money/grants/lmit.shtml#low*.

A typical example family with two children living in Ontario would have to earn less than $43,285 to qualify as low-income, or less than $83,319 to slide in under the middle-income bar (all figures as of

2012). There are significant differences between provinces, so be sure to check what numbers pertain to you (or don't bother, because it's figured out automatically anyway). The good news for you students who have been out of high school for at least four years is that your income will be considered "independent" and, if you make less than $20,000 or so a year, you should qualify as low-income.

What's the benefit of fitting into one of these categories? Well, if your family qualifies for low-income status in the eyes of the powers that be, you are eligible to receive a grant of $250 every month while you are in school full time. Likewise, if you are considered middle-income, you're eligible to receive $100 every month while you're in school full time. The grant program also has specific allowances for students with permanent disabilities, those with dependants, and those enrolled in classes part time (usually a course load of less than sixty percent).

WHY YOU MIGHT BE OUT OF LUCK

One serious flaw in the current student-loan model is the no-man's-land that several students fall into if their parents make a decent chunk of money but, for one reason or another, aren't able or willing to help their children financially through post-secondary schooling. Your parents' income will be considered if you meet either (or both) of the following two conditions:

Condition 1

- You're younger than eighteen.

Condition 2

- You've never been married and have never lived in a long-term common-law relationship (at least twelve months); *and*
- You don't have any dependent children; *and*
- You haven't been out of secondary school for four years (forty-eight months) or more—*or* you haven't been in the workforce for two periods of twelve consecutive months.

If you are considered a dependent student, the federal government and its little provincial-government siblings expect your parents to contribute a fairly healthy amount of their "discretionary income" to help you through your studies. The exact amount depends on such variables as how many children are in your family, how many children in your family are attending post-secondary education, the income levels of both parents, your province of residence, etc. Check out the Parental Contribution Calculator at *tools.canlearn.ca/cslgs-scpse/cln-cln/50/ccp-pcc/af.ccp-pcc_ecran-screen1-eng.do* to see how the formula applies to you. A common complaint across Canada is that a relatively high family income prevents students from obtaining not just Canada student grants, but also any student loans at all.

If you are thinking about misrepresenting any information (i.e., lying) on your student-loan application, you need to know that the Canada Revenue Agency (CRA) does randomly select students for audit every year. "Taking your chances" is illegal; and you could face some fairly stiff penalties, such as being forced to pay back the *entire* loan, *with interest*, *immediately*—or even criminal prosecution if fraud is determined to have been intentional and fairly serious.

If your parents both make decent wages but have decided you need to pay for school independently—well, you're basically out of luck. Flip to Chapter 12 for some other options you may wish to pursue.

APPLYING FOR STUDENT LOANS

Applying for student loans can be a fairly trying and difficult experience, especially your first time around the block. But never fear: we're here to help you iron out the wrinkles.

Before we get into the nuts and bolts of filling out applications, we need to address quickly the provincial differences concerning student-loan applications. Remember that when you apply for student loans you're basically applying for a provincial student loan and a Canada student loan. Student loans are tied to your residency status, and that status is determined by the last province you lived in for twelve consecutive months without attending full-time post-secondary study. Specific and updated information is at *CanLearn.ca*, but here is a summary of how student-loan applications are handled provincially, circa 2012:

- Residents of **Alberta, Manitoba, Nova Scotia**, and **Prince Edward Island** have only to fill out their provincial student-loan forms and then the Canada student loan will be administered with the same information—but the provincial and Canada loans will remain separate entities.

- For residents of **British Columbia, Ontario, New Brunswick, Newfoundland and Labrador**, and **Saskatchewan**, provincial student loans are fully integrated with the federal student-loan program, and the NSLSC handles everything.

- For residents of the **Northwest Territories, Nunavut**, and **Quebec**, Canada student loans are not applicable. These territories and Quebec administer their own student-loan programs, which are totally separate from those of the federal government. You apply for the provincial program only.

- Residents of the **Yukon** have a great grants program that takes the place of provincial student loans. The only student *loans* available to Yukon residents are Canada student loans. Make sure to look into the Yukon grant program though if you've lived there for a couple years.

Now that you can kind of wrap your arms around what a student loan is and where your money will be coming from, you need to make sure you are eligible. Here are the requirements from the Government of Canada; to apply for government student loans and grants, you must do all of the following:

1. Be a Canadian citizen, a permanent resident of Canada, or a protected person.
2. Be a permanent resident of a province or territory that issues government student loans and grants.
3. Demonstrate financial need.
4. Be enrolled in a degree, diploma, or certificate program that runs for at least twelve weeks in a fifteen-week period and is offered by a designated post-secondary institution.
5. Be taking at least 60 percent of a full course load if you're a full-time student, or 20 to 59 percent of a full course load if you're a part-time student.
6. Pass a credit check if you're at least twenty-two and are applying for student loans and grants for the first time.
7. Not have exhausted your maximum lifetime limit of financial assistance, including interest-free status.

GETTING YOUR DUCKS IN A ROW

If you sit down to look at student loans for the first time and try to negotiate a website or forms without getting some information together first, you will be frustrated. Filling out student-loan applications isn't our idea of a good time, but you'll make things a lot easier if you get the following stuff in order before you start (there is nothing like being timed out of your online session eight times while you look for information):

1. Your Social Insurance Number.
2. Your income-tax returns from last year.
3. The revenue you have taken in during the summer (common-

ly called the "pre-study period"). This includes all earnings, government assistance, scholarship income, etc. (but not loans; borrowed money that you have to pay back is not revenue). The number you'll need is the gross income (the number before any deductions are made—not the fact that you earned so little during the summer that it was in fact disgusting). You may have to estimate for the final month of the pre-study period.

4. An estimate of your study-period income, from all sources, for the academic year you're about to embark on. This can be verified at a later date.

5. Records and receipts of moving expenses you incurred, or will incur, when moving to and from your place of study.

6. A complete record of your academic status since the end of high school—when you took courses, whether you were a full-time or part-time student, etc.

7. Your commuting distance to school if you're driving a fair distance daily. (Google Maps is helpful.)

8. A copy of your parents' tax return from last year, if you're considered a dependent student.

9. A copy of your spouse's tax return from last year, if you're married or have common-law status.

10. The account numbers and balances of all your bank accounts. (Your account number is on your cheques for that account.)

11. The details of your RRSPs, trusts, and similar financial instruments, if you have such instruments.

12. The details of any RESP income you will receive during the academic year.

13. The year, make, and model of your vehicle, if you own one.

14. The name and length of your educational program.

15. Your student status for last year and the upcoming year. If you had at least sixty percent of a full course load, you probably were considered a full-time student.

16. The amount of your tuition for the upcoming academic year, including all compulsory fees. For a full description of which compulsory fees are applicable and which aren't, check *CanLearn.ca*. If you've already registered for your courses, the figure should be accessible in your online student-registration account. If you haven't yet registered, the school should be able to able to give you a pretty good estimate: call the Registrar's Office or Administration Centre.

Once you're drowning in this sea of information and are ready to tear up whatever is nearest, you're ready to begin the fun and fulfilling process that is a student-loan application.

As we noted before, not all Canadian students are eligible for student loans. Here's the formula that the government uses to determine whether you get any help:

Allowable Costs – Resources = Assessed Need

On your form, there should be a little description of exactly what constitutes an "allowable cost"; examples might be tuition and compulsory fees, textbooks, computers and related hardware, transportation, living allowances, and child daycare allowances. Resources at a student's disposal might include, but are not necessarily limited to, savings, earnings, RRSPs, trusts, RESP withdrawals, scholarships, vehicle ownership, and parents' income.

The idea of assessed need is based on the minimal amount that you need in order to complete your studies. A student loan is not meant to fund a week at the beach in February. Keep that in mind when you receive your new windfall.

You can get a good estimate of how much your student loan will be, as well as the information involved in determining the amount, at *tools.canlearn.ca/cslgs-scpse/cln-cln/50/sfae-eafe/sfae-eafe-0-eng.do*.

Because your eyes probably glazed over somewhere near the fourth paragraph of this scintillating chapter, here are the short answers to a few frequently asked questions about student loans:

1. If any information you gave when applying for your student loan changes, you're responsible for notifying the relevant administrative organization for your province.

2. Most official sources state that student-loan applications take four to six weeks to process. In our experience, paper applications often take longer than that, but online applications take less than the generalized four to six weeks.

3. You don't receive all of your student loan at once. The normal allocation is sixty percent at the beginning of the first term (usually in October) and forty percent at the beginning of the second term (in late January or in February).

4. Loans typically are meant to help with just one school year's expenses. To get another loan for another year, you'll need to submit a new application.

5. Making early payments toward your loan debt while you are still in school is completely acceptable.

6. There's a process to contest the results of your student-loan application; but the rules are applied pretty stringently, in our experience. We have heard from some student-loan officials that there are cases in which more loan funding is made available. If you think your case warrants a second look, we recommend that you start by contacting your provincial student-loan office.

KEEP IN MIND . . .

When you're applying for student loans we can't emphasize enough how important it is to be organized and to submit your application well before the deadline. The earlier you get the ball rolling on this stuff, the easier it will be. Students who miss deadlines and are counting on the funding can end up in world of hurt. If there is one thing we learned while going through post-secondary education, it is not to depend on bureaucracies to handle forms properly and efficiently. Give yourself a "buffer" in case something gets mixed up or "lost in the mail".

One hidden benefit of student loans, and the reason why we now recommend that many people apply for them even if they're going to get only a very small amount of money, is that getting a loan opens up a world of extra opportunities for scholarships, bursaries, and grants. Many of these awards require a student to "demonstrate financial need". What that almost always means is that you need to have a student loan of some kind that you can show as proof that you are in financial need. At many institutions, there are even awards that are given *automatically* (*if* you apply) on the basis of financial need and GPA or another criterion. Check out Chapter 3, on scholarships, bursaries, and grants, for more information.

REPAYING STUDENT LOANS

The cap and gown fit nicely, and everyone wants to shake your hand; you go to a ceremony and listen to the same twenty cliché metaphors that every graduate endures—and then suddenly you're pushed out of your cozy confines of post-secondary education and into the not so warm embrace of the working world. Now what? At the end of the day, someone has to pay the piper, as the saying goes, and in this case the piper is pretty adamant that the bill will be paid! Student-loan debt is notoriously difficult to squirm your way out of, and even if you declare most types of bankruptcy it will still follow you around (this is to prevent the obvious scenario in which every student who has debt simply declares bankruptcy upon stepping into the "real world"). If you refuse to pay your student loans (i.e., if you **default** on them), your credit score will take a massive hit. This might not matter much to you now, but a low credit score means banks might not lend you money to buy a car or a house and, if they do, they will make you pay crazy-high interest rates. Let's just say "dining and dashing" is not an option here.

When you finish your studies, you will have to make a few decisions about how you will repay that chunk of money you borrowed. To put it in terms that the average eighteen-year-old might understand: this is the Sunday morning after the party of the year, buddy. Actually, it's not all that bad. Basically, after you leave post-secondary education, you have to decide the following questions:

1. When will you start paying your loans back?
2. What method will you use to make your loan payments every month?
3. What type of interest rate will you choose for your loans?
4. Over what length of time will you repay your loans, and how much will you pay every month?

Depending on which province you live in, different rules apply (see page 74 for how each province administers its financial aid). When you've finished school, almost all student loans include some sort of grace period to let you get on your feet and find work. For the Canada student loans, this grace period means that you don't have to make any payments for six months, but interest on the money you borrowed will begin to accumulate immediately. The provincial rules vary a little, but the same principle applies. You don't have to take advantage of the grace period; it's just an option.

There is a variety of ways in which you can repay your student loan after you leave school, and the choice is yours. *You are responsible for setting up a program to repay the money that you borrowed.* Usually the student-loan administrators will give you notice either by phone or email, but it's still up to you to follow their directions and set up your payment plan. If you fail to do this, payments will be taken automatically out of the account that you had the original loan deposited into. If there is no money in that account, please, re-read this section and pay attention to the word *default* ("Do not pass go, do not collect $200"). While you can choose to write a cheque every month, almost all young people these days take advantage of the efficiency of automatic payment plans, in which their loan payments are taken out of their bank accounts every month without any further human input. This eliminates a lot of paperwork, not to mention the risk of forgetting about the manual process of writing a cheque.

INTEREST RATES

Welcome to the world of interest rates. Interest rates are powerful forces of nature that can make you rich if you make them work for you—or can cripple you if you fail to harness their power. If you're thinking this sounds like some sort of black magic from Game of Thrones, you aren't far off. More Canadians understand science fiction than how interest rates work! As far as your Canada student loans are concerned, there is only one choice you have to make:

- **Option 1.** The amount you borrowed will be subject to a variable interest rate of prime plus 2.5 percent.
- **Option 2.** The amount you borrowed will be subject to a fixed interest rate of prime plus 5 percent.

Your provincial student loans probably have similar options, but the details depend on where you borrowed the money. Some provinces have even begun allowing students to repay the provincial part of their loans at a flat prime rate.

We know many of you probably got nervous while reading that "banker's speak", but it's pretty straightforward. The term *prime* means the **prime interest rate** that the Bank of Canada sets every three months. This is sort of the baseline for any loan you take out. The terms *variable* and *fixed* describe whether or not you lock in your interest rate at a specific number. Because the prime rate can move up and down, you can choose to lock in your loan at the current rate plus 5 percent for the life of your loan and you will know exactly how much you will pay every month (it won't ever change). For example, if you lock in a fixed rate when prime is 3 percent, your interest rate will always be 8 percent (3 + 5). If you choose the variable rate, it will "float" with the prime rate and always stay 2.5 percent above whatever prime happens to be at any given moment. In other words, if you choose the reliability of a fixed rate, you pay extra for the guarantee; that's why it's prime plus 5 percent instead of prime plus 2.5 percent.

We Canadians are a weird people in how much we treasure the security of fixed interest rates. In choosing between these two options, you will probably hear numerous smart people give you completely different advice. For what it's worth, in broad studies of mortgage loans, variable rates save people money about ninety percent of the time. That being said, interest rates are unusually low right now (2012) and some people suggest that this means you should lock in your rate before rates rise to a more normal range. The truth is that no one has any idea what the prime interest rate will do more than two years from now—and anyone who does is going to keep it secret and make a huge profit on it. For our money, we're fairly certain that the vast majority of students would be better off with a "floating" or variable rate—but there is always the chance that interest rates will quickly rise and make that opinion look dumb. Even if you don't take the path we suggest, the silver lining is that you could flip a coin and be just as smart as the "experts" who will tell you they know where the interest rates will be ten years from now.

The final decision you have to make about your student loans is how you organize your payment schedule. The default option, which most students choose, is paying back the loan over ten years, including the grace period. If you want to be out of debt faster, you can choose a shorter period, and the total amount you'll pay in interest will be lower, but then obviously you will have to pay more per month. An important consideration is that you can choose to raise your monthly payment at any point—and you can make a lump-sum payment whenever you want as well. Given that fact, we suggest setting up a basic ten-year plan and then just making larger payments if you decide you want to at any point. There is no penalty for that. It's also interesting to ask your bank to show you the different numbers for paying off the loan bi-weekly and for paying it off monthly. If you repay the loan bi-weekly, you will whittle down the principal faster and pay less interest. Also, remember that, if your loan was from certain provinces, you will be paying off the provincial student loan and the Canada student loan separately, so you'll have to make two sets of arrangements.

REPAYMENT ASSISTANCE PLAN

In case you're having trouble repaying your student loans and feel as if you're about to drown, there are some life-preservers available to you. Starting in 2009, the federal government started a program called the Repayment Assistance Plan (RAP). (In case you didn't notice, calling a government program by the acronym *RAP* is their way of trying to stay "hip" and connect with the youth of today.) If you apply for this program, you may be eligible for help, in the form of interest relief and debt reduction, depending on your income level and employment status. Similar help exists if you have a permanent disability. At any point, borrowers of student loans can look at revising the terms of their loans and there may be some help available from either the federal or provincial government. We recommend applying for help before you're in a financial crisis, so that there will be time to stave off Armageddon for your credit rating and bank account.

PAYING STUDENT-LOAN INTEREST CAN MAKE ME MONEY?

One cool thing about student loans that you might not care about now, but which you will care about in a few years, is that the interest you pay on them is eligible for a federal tax credit—and probably a provincial tax credit too. This means that, because you paid interest on your student loans during the year, both your provincial and federal governments will give you money back in your tax refund. See CHAPTER 9 for more information.

Chapter 7 Summary

- Despite what you may have heard, student loans are actually a pretty good deal.
- Canada Student Grants are money that is given (as opposed to lent) to you on the basis of your assessed need.
- Not every student can get Canada student loans. Certain eligibility requirements must be met and you must have an assessed need according to this formula:

  Allowable Costs – Resources = Assessed Need
- Every province has unique student-loan rules that you need to pay attention to.
- If you prepare properly for doing your student-loan application, you'll almost certainly find it faster and much less frustrating than if you don't get things ready first.
- Having a student loan opens up many different scholarship and bursary options that are based on financial need.
- Repaying student loans is not optional, and it is your responsibility to set up your repayment plans. Being aware of terms and options makes this much easier.

CHAPTER EIGHT

SUMMER JOBS AND PART-TIME WORK

IN days of yore, post-secondary students would get off school in May, or even late April, and find "college jobs" painting houses, waiting tables, or life-guarding, and this would give them enough money to pay their tuition—and most of their living expenses, in case they didn't live at home. Today's student doesn't get to live that fairy tale. With the rise in tuition far outpacing general inflation, the question of balancing work and study while in school is an important one for young people.

The first thing we would advise students to consider is that there is no one-size-fits-all piece of advice that will work for everyone when it comes to finding the premium balance of a social life, cracking the books, and earning a paycheque (oh, and sleep . . . maybe). We've seen students succeed who decided to work part-time all year round while taking courses in the spring and summer sessions (probably an under-used strategy). We've also seen students pick careers that they knew would be high-paying and not worry much about taking out a few extra grand in student loans if that allowed them to achieve better balance while in school. Then there are those lucky few whose parents can afford to pay for their whole schooling journey, and who therefore can focus on building résumés, as opposed to merely earning a little cash.

Both of us took fairly traditional paths when it came to employment options. We were each able to earn and save a substantial amount of money over the summer months and, when we combined that with the rest of our bag of financial tricks, we were able to avoid having to work "real jobs" during the school year. Many students today are not as fortunate as we were (although there are a few ways to tilt the summer-employment table in your favour, which we'll get to in a moment). A higher percentage of post-secondary students than ever before are working during the school year. This probably is partly because of the disruption of many traditional patterns of summer work. In 2008 (back when Drake was still a dorky kid battling acne problems on a mediocre CBC show), the full-time summer employment rate for post-secondary students was around 70 percent, which was considered fairly normal at the time. As of 2010, students' full-time summer employment rate had sunk to 51.8 percent, with just 66.4 percent of students finding employment at all, whether full-time or not; the average hours were 27.7 a week; and the average hourly wage was $12.80. If the average summer lasts eighteen weeks and we use the numbers from 2010, the average student has a gross summer income around $6,400. These numbers, generated in the aftermath of a recession in our workforce, paint a somewhat bleak picture for post-secondary students. Unless you live at home, those earnings just aren't going to cut it as far as covering basic expenses.

Even though those averages can be depressing, there certainly are ways to boost your summer earnings and give yourself a better chance of building up a solid billfold before the first week of classes. Among the advantages that working during the summer gave us was that it allowed us to get involved with a ton of extracurricular stuff during the school year (which eventually ended up on our résumés and helped us get jobs). It also made it easier for us to take heavier course loads. Doing that means fewer years in school and more time in the workforce. We know that, for many students, not having a part-time job to split their focus during the school year allowed them to concentrate on achieving their full academic potential. (That sounded really teacher-ish, didn't it?) This academic focus led to more scholarships and to entrance into high-competition faculties. For example, Kyle was able to live at home while working his summer job and, thanks to his parents' rent-equals-chores policy, every summer he was able to bank some solid coin in preparation for the school year. This is a sweet deal if you can swing it. If you use the strategy of going home to find summer work, paying living expenses for only eight months of the year can really cut down on the budget squeeze.

Kyle's summer-job experience was in working for the Canada Border Service Agency as a Student Border Guard. Yes, he was one of those distinguished individuals whose job was to inconvenience people who were innocent ninety-nine percent of the time. Not only did the job give him some great résumé material and work experience that could be applied in a variety of contexts: it also gave him a decent paycheque. Back in the Stone Age (2006), when he started his first summer of work, the base pay was $11.16 an hour. While that doesn't seem spectacular, you have to remember that you could buy a pop and bag of chips for a quarter back in those days. (O.K., so it wasn't *that* long ago—but wages were a little lower on average back then.) With shift premiums and seniority bonuses, Kyle probably averaged around $18 an hour in his final summer there, in 2009. The shift work also allowed him to pick up some one-off jobs on the side to supplement his income during the summer months. All told, his gross wages were $11,000 to $17,000, per summer, during his years at the border.

Justin landed an optimal summer position for himself as a marketing-representative assistant at the agricultural giant known as Macdon Industries. The company manufactures farm machinery, such a swathers and combine parts. His job was to travel around (on the company dime, of course) and put on presentations for equipment dealers, showcasing the unique features of Macdon's products. Justin raves about the experience, saying that he made some decent money (about $9,000 to $13,000, each summer) and got some great experience in the industry he thought he might be going into. Even better than making a ton of money: he got to *save* a lot of money *while also travelling* all over North America; and, because all of his expenses were paid by his employer, he never had a chance to spend his paycheque on the usual summer temptations. Justin also credits this job with building up his "soft skills", such as public speaking and working with others in many different environments; there is no doubt that this helped him as he made the leap into the workforce.

So how do you get a great summer job that will give you skills *and* pay the bills? We actually believe that it isn't that hard: you just have to be willing to make a few sacrifices. Here are some summer-job-seeking tactics that we consistently saw work during our time in university for people of all backgrounds, and ones that we used effectively:

1. Start Looking Early

Despite what students today tell us, we're not actually contemporaries of the dinosaurs and we do remember what it's like to perfect the art of procrastination when you're in school. Don't fall into this imperceptible trap. When students think great summer jobs will just fall into their laps at the end of April (a time when everyone else is also looking for summer work), it reminds us of an ostrich sticking its head in the ground, thinking no one can see it. Remember, no one owes you a job: you have to differentiate yourself from the pack if you don't want to hear "Sorry; we decided to go in another direction." To land a great summer job, you have to start looking early. November is not too early. The summer before is not too early. There is no "too early"! The more groundwork you're able to put in place early in the school year, the better your chances will be come April and May.

2. Keep an Open Mind

Don't dismiss whole categories of jobs without looking into them a little. So many people see a job posting like "Garbage Collector" or the famous "Student Pro Painter" ads and immediately dismiss it as being "beneath" them. We'll never understand this logic. You are an entry-level employee, so, please, don't have preconceived notions about what you are "above" doing! Often these jobs that not many people want have decent paycheques attached, specifically because there has to be something to entice applicants and keep the employees on: that's the beauty of this whole supply-and-demand, free-market thing we have going.

3. Be Willing to Travel

Perhaps the single most important factor we have seen in consistently getting well-paying summer jobs is that they are often found far from urban centres. We're rural kids, so for us this wasn't a big deal; but, for many students, leaving their friends and home for a few months is quite intimidating. Try to see it as an opportunity: think of all the exotic stories you'll have to tell when you get back! Most of the jobs we've gotten have been ours at least partly because we were willing to work in rural areas. Whether it's a government position planting trees, holding a stop sign at a road construction site, or a geological surveying job, a rural job pays to get you out there, and it's really not that bad. We promise. In fact, if you give wide open spaces, clean air, serene landscapes, and country charm a chance, they just might grow on you!

4. Cast a Wide Net

When you start looking for summer jobs (repeat after us: "Never Too Early"), don't just Google "Summer Jobs <Insert Town Name Here>" and look at the first page of results. The Internet is a great resource, but it is limited in terms of the personal connection that can often be the key to getting you a job. Let your friends and relatives know you're looking for a job, and keep an open mind. Often, a softly spoken word here or there can be enough to land you the gig, or at least get you on the right track.

5. Ingratiate Yourself before Summer Comes

Whether you intern, volunteer, or work part time at a potential employer's business after the first semester, just getting your face in the workplace and showing some initiative will separate you from the pack. Don't be a nuisance, but do offer to get your training done early (or something similar) so that you can hit the ground running as soon as school is done. Offering to shadow someone on weekends is another good way to get your foot in the door and earn yourself the "go-getter" label.

6. Create Your Own Position

If you don't like what's out there, summon your inner entrepreneurial spirit and make something happen for yourself. For example, we've seen several self-made landscapers do quite well for themselves. The final summer before Kyle began teaching, he created a position at a boxing gym where he had trained for a few years. The first step was to ask the owners and coaches of the non-profit enterprise whether they'd be open to creating a summer position for youth programming if he got government funding to cover most of his salary. The management there basically said "Show us a proposal and the potential funding" ("Show me the money!"—love *Jerry Maguire*). Kyle dressed up the program a little, mentioned he had a bachelor's degree in education, and was approved by the Urban Green Team (government funding). The guys who ran the gym were so impressed that they topped up his wages so that he was making roughly $15 an hour, which was great for teaching kids how to box, as far as he was concerned! Even more rewarding for Kyle was the fact that he got to build a program from the ground up—and leave detailed instructions so that the program could continue to grow. Making your own way is really not that hard: it just takes a little creativity and verve.

WORKING DURING THE SCHOOL YEAR

If the summer job circuit just isn't kind to you even after you implement our tips, try something we've have seen many people do: they free up time for work during the school year by taking a summer course or two. We know—school in the summer sucks. But almost every study we've read in the education world says that we retain information much better if we keep learning and reading over the summer (without long breaks of two to four months). Taking a summer course or two can give you an open slot during the rest of the year for work, to make up for not scraping together enough moolah during the summer. Many students even choose to pursue their most difficult or time-consuming course during the summer, when they can focus on it fairly exclusively: it's a solid plan with which to attack the GPA game.

If you add up your costs for the coming school year and find that your expected income from your summer job, parental help, and scholarships and bursaries just won't be enough for all your necessary expenses, your best options to make up the difference are the aforementioned student loans and working during the school year. In 2009–2010, Canadian students aged twenty to twenty-four who worked during the school year earned, on average, about $7,000. Students under twenty earned a little less and had a harder time finding work. These earnings don't come without sacrifice, however. A recent Statistics Canada report by Katherine Marshall, "Employment Patterns of Postsecondary Students", came to some interesting conclusions. The report states that growing numbers of students choose to work during the school year, and that there's consensus among academics that long hours at work during the school year almost certainly hurt student performance (duh). Findings were less conclusive when students worked fewer hours, at part-time jobs. Basically, from what we could gather, after much money was spent and people smarter than we are looked at the issues surrounding more students' trying to work more hours during the school year in a tough labour environment, the grand conclusion was—drum roll—Don't overdo it!

Now, we don't pretend to be experts on finding jobs while simultaneously taking courses, or even on which jobs are better than others, because, really, to be honest, we never tried to balance things that way. But you don't exist in the hallowed halls of post-secondary education for seven years without picking up a few things from others' experience. When you're thinking about balancing your academic, social, and work lives, it's worth noting that professors and other "experts" state that you should be putting in two hours of homework for every hour that you're in class. In our experience, the validity of this rule of thumb depends highly on your specific faculty and field of study.

Some of the best options we saw work well for people involved finding jobs on campus. Any place where thousands of people converge every day is going to create some employment possibilities. Once you get your foot in the door behind the scenes on campus, you have access to a huge network of connections. You can quickly find your way into a position that fits your wants and needs. Campus jobs have a built-in advantage in that the bosses, who know students have unique schedules, are often much more flexible with hours than off-campus employers are. Another big advantage of working on campus is that you don't have to factor any additional travel time and expense into your budget, because you're already travelling to campus every day anyway. For many students, trying to get across town to another job can be a time-consuming struggle, especially if they rely on public transportation. Burning $10 and an extra two hours every work day in order to make $12 a shift probably isn't a great idea in terms of creating balance for yourself. Finally, on-campus work usually offers pretty good pay for entry-level employees—almost always solidly above minimum wage. Here are just some of the jobs and workplaces suitable for students on campus:

Administration assistant	Mail centre
Book store	Resident adviser
Copy centre	Security
Daycare centre	Special-events staff
Food services	Student Council or Student Union
Gym	Teaching assistant
Intramural referee	Technical assistant (audio/visual)
Lab assistant	Tour guide
Library	Tutor
Lifeguard	Youth programming

There are literally thousands of jobs available on many campuses across Canada. Many colleges and universities are like small towns and offer a full variety of jobs just waiting for you!

Sometimes the on-campus options just don't work out or you may simply choose to pursue a job off campus. When wandering off campus to find work, keep in mind the costs, in terms of money spent on travel and the strain that commuting will put on your daily schedule. Remember, the key here is your ability to manage your limited amount of time in a way that allows you to earn a little cash and doesn't cripple your academics or your social life (if you're one of those weird students who are into something other than work and study). Some common options are work in the service industry and the retail sector. We know waiters and waitresses who make pretty good earnings when their tips are included; but you should be prepared to start at minimum wage if you're looking for part-time work off campus.

Offering advice on part-time jobs that is broadly applicable is very difficult, because everyone's situation is unique. Some people are just able to balance things more easily than others because their academic schedules are less demanding or because their time-management skills are simply better. We also know that working a minimum-wage job to feed party habits or to take a couple grand off of your student loans probably isn't worth it if it's going to hurt your academic standing. If earning just a few thousand bucks at an entry-level job during the school year forces you to drop classes and take an extra year or two in order to graduate, the math simply doesn't add up. You should be able to make substantially more money working at a full-time job once you have post-secondary credentials than you would at a part-time job without those credentials. The other consideration, in terms of your academic standing, is the idea that the hours you spend at work might be the very hours you need to put into attaining a high GPA to get into that specific faculty you want, such as law, dentistry, or pharmacy.

Whether you're considering summer jobs or part-time work during the school year, remember that, although those dollar signs might look big at the moment, the real value lies in setting yourself up for the longer term. No matter where you end up, treat people well and stay in touch. These connections will become extremely valuable when you look to enter the workforce for the long haul. We're sure you've heard the cliché "It's not what you know, but who you know." We cannot overemphasize the degree to which this statement is true. Especially in economic climates such as the one we are in today, with relatively high unemployment rates, your personal network of connections is incredibly valuable. Trying to get a job by mailing out a few résumés or typing up a quick online application simply doesn't cut it anymore, no matter whether it's a summer job or a long-term position after your post-secondary education.

In some cases, we recommend taking a pay cut, or even looking at an unpaid internship and volunteering, if it means gaining valuable skills, experience, and connections that you can use to your advantage later in your career. In our opinion, having a few thousand dollars in student debt is sometimes blown out of proportion, compared to the lifelong earning potential that can be built up while you're in post-secondary education. When you have earned your degree, diploma, or certificate, would you rather have nothing in the bank and no job experience, leading to no decent job opportunities, or would you rather owe a few grand in student loans but take your pick of jobs because of the experience and personal connections you have gained? While the real-life question is rarely that simple, and the ideal obviously is to find a great-paying job that allows you to get relevant experience too, the scenario we recommend is definitely a consideration that too many students ignore in favour of focusing on "the here and now".

As you proceed through your education, you'll probably grow ever more comfortable with what works for you in terms of finding a balance of work, study, and play. Just remember to keep your eye on your final goals in terms of not only earning money to stay out of debt but also the long-term considerations. Please, check out Appendix A and Appendix B for résumé and interview tips that will help you land that perfect job that you have your eye on, whether it's part-time, full-time seasonal, or a stepping-stone in your future career.

Chapter 8 Summary

- Finding the right balance between school and work to fit your wants and needs is highly personal, and someone else's ideal mix might not work for you.
- There are several proven strategies you can use to increase your chances of landing a good job. *Note:* Opportunities won't just fall into your lap!
- Working on campus can be a great option for part-time work during the school year.
- Keep in mind that finding a job that can further your career can be worth a lot in the long term.

CHAPTER NINE

FREE MONEY WHEN YOU NEED IT MOST (STUDENT TAX RETURNS)

WHO wants free money? Who wants free money during the spring, when most students are buying discount noodles and "red sauce" to get by?

(*Now doesn't that sound way more enticing than a "Student Tax Returns" chapter?*)

When we were eighteen, the word *taxes* meant something that was taken from our paycheques for no real reason that we could see, and filing was something our parents took care of for us when we got some magic slip of paper called a T4 in the mail. We have glorious news for students everywhere: taxes aren't that hard! There are only about ten or fifteen real things you need to know when doing your taxes as a student, and there is free software out there that you can use to do your taxes in about an hour. You may not believe us yet—but take five minutes to read the rest of this chapter and see whether you still feel the need to be one of "those people" who stumble over to a tax-preparation place the day before taxes are due, only to stand in line for three hours and then pay someone to ask them the exact same prompts they would have been asked if they had simply downloaded the free software.

(*Important note:* We're definitely not tax professionals (and we didn't even stay at a Holiday Inn Express last night), so we strongly recommend consulting someone with the right credentials, or the Canada Revenue Agency's website, *cra-arc.gc.ca*, if you have any questions or concerns.)

Getting the most free money out of your tax returns is a simple process (actually, it's basically your money you're just getting back anyway), yet it's one that intimidates us because of our general aversion to the math and weird terminology that exist in the tax industry. Honestly, if you stay organized throughout the year, and then answer the basic prompts on the free or cheap student tax software so readily available, just about all of you will be able to get back everything your government owes you. Indeed, your government wants to help you and other students and therefore has included a few cool little things in the tax code for you to take advantage of.

Given our lack of knowledge when we were eighteen, we won't assume that everyone knows how the income-tax system works. Here are the basics. Let's say you work a job for $15 an hour, and you work ten hours in a week. That makes for $150 a week, which is your **gross pay**. But the paycheque you get for that week is probably for less than $150. That's because money that you are assumed to owe in various **payroll taxes** is set aside for the government. (If it weren't set aside from the very beginning, you might spend it all, forget all about taxes, and have no money left to pay your taxes when they come due next year.) The amounts that are set aside before you can cash or deposit your cheque are called **payroll deductions**. The amount of money your cheque is actually made out for (after the deductions have been taken care of) is your **net pay**. (There are ways to ask that no money be deducted from your cheque; if you're interested in that option, see page 108 and visit *cra-arc.gc.ca*.) Some deductions, such as your contributions to employment insurance (EI) and Canadian Pension Plan (CPP), are money that you cannot get back. But, generally, the parts that are labelled "Provincial Income Tax" and "Federal Income Tax" are amounts that you, as a student, will be able to recoup.

How does the government determine how much tax you should pay? It's based on your job earnings, how many dependants you have, and a slew of other considerations. Every year, Canadians are obligated to fill out tax forms that show how much money they made in the previous year, how much tax they paid (this is shown on the document called a T4, provided by employers), and what deductions and credits they're entitled to. Filling out those forms tells you either how much the government needs to give back to you, or how much you owe the government on top of all the taxes that were taken from your paycheques throughout the year.

This process would be rather hard if you had to learn how to navigate tax forms, but the great part is that today's software takes care of that for you. We won't recommend one student tax software program over another, but if you check at your student-union office when tax time rolls around there are usually some free options available. They all use basically the same process. The software prompts you with a question, such as "Are you single or married?" or "Did you receive any scholarships or bursaries this year?" You simply answer the question, and the program handles which box to put your answer in on the form. Then you just follow the directions to send your taxes through the NETFILE system to the Canadian government—and wait for the money to come.

Whether you file the old fashioned way with a paper and pen, or online, you don't have to wait for the deadline to do your tax return: if you really need the money in February or early March, go ahead and file.

We believe students (and everyone else for that matter) should try doing their own taxes at least once, whether it's on paper or electronically. If you still think it isn't worth your time, try to find a private person to do them. The extra $20 you'll pay above the common strip-mall retail operation's rate will probably be recouped in tax savings. Nearly every single student we ever talked to who went to one of these large branch locations had the same story, and it's one we experienced too. The people at the company assume (and are usually right) that, because you're a student, they won't make much money off of you (especially because the fee they charge you is a flat rate, not commission-based compensation)—so they put you with seasonal employees, who were just brought in to help with tax season. Often, these people are not well trained, and all they do is read you the same prompts that the free software would have given you. Many students who go to these large companies also choose to get their tax-refund money immediately—for which they pay the company a percentage of the eventual cheque that comes from the government. This is a terrible deal, and it takes advantage of students' financial illiteracy and the immediate need for cash that most students feel every spring.

But we're here to help you take control of your own finances. Read the fourteen tips below, and get your money back.

1. Tax Credits and Tax Deductions

There are two basic terms that will you help you understand your taxes better (but you don't even need to know these to do your taxes with free software). The terms are *tax credit* and *tax-deductible expense*, and they are the two main ways to lower the amount of tax you owe when you're a student.

Tax credits are set amounts that the government gives back to you through your tax refund if you meet certain criteria. The amount is determined by multiplying the amount of the tax credit by the lowest federal tax rate (fifteen percent) and refunding the resulting amount of money to you. Each of the provincial tax credits works similarly to the federal ones.

A **tax-deductible expense** is something whose cost the government pretends was not part of your income if you spent money on it. Confused? Here's an example. Let's say your gross income one year is $20,000. (Remember, gross income is all of your income before taxes and other things are subtracted from it.) Normally, if your gross income were $20,000, the government would say that you owed a specific amount of money in taxes because you had taken in $20,000. But now let's add to the picture: during the year when you earned $20,000, you took $3,000 from your $20,000 income and you spent that $3,000 on a tax-deductible expense. In that case, you would deduct the $3,000 from $20,000, and then the result ($17,000) would be the only part of your income that would be taxed. You wouldn't hand over as many dollars in taxes for an income of $17,000 as you would for an income of $20,000.

Students get to make great use out of both of these tools—credits and deductions.

All of the following tax tips on this list are applicable to your federal tax return. Each province has its own student tax-credit rules and, while we've mentioned a few of them, it's a fairly safe bet that your software program will ask you questions specific to the province you live in.

2. Get Organized!

You will need the slip called a T4 (Statement of Remuneration Paid—a fancy way of saying "what you earned") from every employer you had during the year. You will also need a document called a T2202A from your place of post-secondary education (this is for tips 4, 5, and 6, coming up). Besides these two documents, you may need some sort of documentation concerning your housing situation and the rent that you paid. It is also a good idea to keep your major receipts, and receipts from charitable donations, or really any receipt for that matter! No one ever got in trouble for keeping too many of them. On the other hand, people often lose out on tax savings because of receipts they lost or consciously filed in the recycling bin. Once you get used to keeping it all together, it's not hard to look through quickly at tax time.

3. Scholarships, Bursaries, and Grants

Gather the information on the financial awards that you received. The tax rules for these have been changing in recent years, and you now have to report them as income (you'll get a T4A, showing them as part of your income); but they all are income that you don't have to pay taxes on.

4. Textbook Tax Credit

The federal government and most provincial governments are cool enough to give you tax credits for your textbooks. The set rates for full-time students and part-time students are calculated automatically. You shouldn't have to produce textbook receipts for the Canada Revenue Agency; but, again, saving receipts in a shoe box or Tupperware container is never a bad idea.

5. Education Tax Credit

The Canadian tax man will also give you a tax credit of $400 for every month of full-time study, and $120 per month of part-time study, provided that the education lasts at least three weeks and is at least twelve hours per month. This is the education tax credit. It's one of those tax credits we were talking about a little bit ago—a specific amount of money that the government just gives right back to you in your tax refund each year. It's a nice little chunk of change for most students. See your Administration office for what constitutes a full-time or part-time course load at your post-secondary institution. You cannot claim the education credit if you received a grant; you also can't claim the education credit if your employer paid for your classes.

6. Tuition Tax Credit

In addition to the flat education and textbook tax credits, which work on the same formula for every student in Canada, the federal government also has a tuition tax credit. Your school website probably lets you log in to print a form for this. Called a T2202A, the form should state the amount you're allowed to use for the tax credit. According to the Canada Revenue Agency, the following expenses *can* be used as part of your tuition tax credit:

a. admission fees
b. charges for use of the library or laboratory facilities
c. exemption fees
d. examination fees (including re-reading charges)
e. application fees (but only if you subsequently enrol in the institution)
f. confirmation fees
g. charges for a certificate, diploma, or degree
h. membership or seminar fees that are specifically related to an academic program and its administration
i. mandatory computer-service fees
j. academic fees.

When the Goods and Services Tax (GST) is added to an eligible tuition fee, the total amount (the fee *plus* the GST) is eligible for the tuition tax credit.

The following fees *cannot* be claimed as part of the tuition tax credit:

a. student activities, whether social or athletic
b. medical care and health services
c. transportation and parking
d. board and lodging
e. goods of enduring value that are to be retained by students (e.g. slide rule, microscope, uniform, gown, etc.)
f. initiation fees and entrance fees to professional organizations
g. administrative penalties incurred when the student withdraws from a program or an institution.

Both of the above lists come almost verbatim from the Canada Revenue Agency. For more specifics about what can and can't be claimed for the tuition tax credit, go to *cra-arc.gc.ca*.

7. Taxes and RESPs

If you have RESP income from your parents, only the educational-assistance payments (EAPs) from the RESP are taxable. In other words, the original amount that your parents put in for you is tax-free in your hands (your parents already paid taxes on it once). The amount that the government put into the plan (commonly called the Canada Education Savings Grant, or CESG), and the earned investment income, are taxable when you take them out. Most software programs will ask you about this. The financial institution that administers your RESP should send your parents a statement that shows how much of the income that you got from the plan is taxable. Are your parents having you read this book? Then *you* should have *them* look at *The RESP Book*, by Mike Holman, which will answer just about any question you and your family have about RESPs.

8. Moving Tax Credit

In a bid to help students with their transportation needs, and to encourage greener living, the government has made transit passes into a non-refundable tax credit. A **non-refundable tax credit** is much the same as the regular old tax credit we discussed at the beginning of the chapter, but it cannot be used to bring the balance of your taxes below zero; check the GLOSSARY for a fuller explanation. Keep track of your public-transit costs (whether they involve a bus pass, a light-rail transit pass, or anything similar) and save your receipt, so that the full amount of this will be granted as a tax credit.

9. Tax-Free Withdrawals from RRSPs

This tip is mostly applicable to older students, those who have already been in the workforce and contributed to RRSPs. As a student, you're allowed to make tax-free withdrawals from your RRSPs to pay for your schooling, under the Lifelong Learning Plan (LLP).

You're allowed to withdraw no more than $10,000 per year, and no more than $20,000 over four years. Also, you must repay this amount, back into your RRSP, within ten years. If you don't proceed with the education program after using the LLP, you need to repay the full amount in the year in which you withdrew the money, or else it'll be taxed as any other income would be.

10. Medical Costs

There are tax breaks for money spent on travelling for medical reasons. The same is true for certain prescription medications. There are many rules concerning medical tax deductions, but any tax software should prompt you about them, and you can get a full breakdown using any search engine and the Canada Revenue Agency if you really want to know what you're entitled to. And, of course, students aren't the only people for whom this point is applicable.

11. Charitable Donations

Our government wants you to give money to charities. If you donate money to a cause, hang on to the receipt that they give you and you can get a nice little chunk of that money back at tax time. Another option that some people take advantage of is to donate items such as old cars and furniture to charity, and use the receipts to save money on taxes. Again, the tax software will ask you for the amount you donated, and it will take care of the rest!

12. Rental Deductions

In certain provinces (Manitoba, Ontario, and Quebec, at the time of this writing), a tax credit is available for people who rent or own their primary residence. This is the **education property tax credit** or **property tax credit**. Students who live on campus in those provinces are considered renters, and they get documentation from the administration in order to claim the tax credit. If you're renting a place off campus, get your landlord to provide you with documentation of your total rent for the year.

13. Child-Care Expenses

If you or your spouse paid for child-care services so that you could earn income or go to school, you're in line for a tax deduction or a tax credit. The child must be under sixteen. Many campuses now have daycare available. Just remember to save your receipts!

14. Why Wait until April to Get Your Money?

Many people don't realize that, when they get a nice tax refund from the government, they're actually just getting their own money back. Now, some students are better off not getting a cheque until they really need that money, in the spring. (We're looking at you, Broke-by-Thanksgiving crowd.) Others would rather have their gross income, without deductions being taken immediately from every paycheque, so they can budget for the year. If you want to pursue this option, just ask for a TD1 form and a T1213 form from your employer. Once you fill in your expected income and your tax credits, the result should be very little tax taken from your paycheque. If you have trouble with budgeting and are intimidated by tax forms, this is not necessarily a great option, because there's always the danger of spending everything you get and then actually owing money at tax time.

AFTER GRADUATION

Here are three points worth keeping in mind.

- If you have graduated recently and have had to start repaying student loans, provincial and federal tax credits are available for the interest you've paid on those loans. Because of the tax-deductibility status of student loans, some smart people prefer to put their paycheque towards other endeavours for the first few years they work. Paying back credit-card debt and lines of credit should definitely come before putting any extra money towards student loans. There is also a solid argument to be made for beginning to save for a house down-payment, or even beginning retirement savings, as opposed to focusing on paying down your student debt. This subject is much debated by finance enthusiasts, but they agree on one thing: you're crazy if you're paying student loans and not getting the tax break designed to help recent graduates. Keep this in mind for the future if you have taken out student loans.

- Many provinces now have tuition-payback tax incentives to encourage you to work in the province where you earned your degree or diploma. This is so that the province can benefit from the training it funded when you were in school. In Manitoba, for example, ten percent of your total tuition costs will be paid back to you each year, for up to six years, through a tax refund.
- If you do not use the tuition, education, and textbook tax credits, you can let your parents or spouse use them. You can also "carry them forward" to a year when you have more income that has been taxed. A couple of years when Kyle was in school, he allowed his parents to claim the credits. It seemed only fair, considering all the ways they were supporting him! We definitely recommend carrying forward at least some of the amounts in your last few years, in preparation for your first year out of post-secondary education, when you'll really need the big tax refund to pay for the seemingly endless barrage of expenses.

We cannot overemphasize the importance of basic organization. The time, money, and effort that are saved by people who get into productive habits, such as keeping bills in a file folder and having a container for major-purchase receipts, is enormous. Save yourself a ton of frustration as you start to get more and more documents in your life to keep track of: GET ORGANIZED! The boys and girls over at the Canada Revenue Agency (CRA) say that you should keep your tax records for the past six years, in case they choose to take a closer look at your situation through a tax audit. If you have any questions on student income taxes and the most recent changes, see the *Students and Income Tax* pamphlet provided (and updated yearly) by the CRA; it's at *cra-arc.gc.ca/E/pub/tg/p105/.*

Chapter 9 Summary

- Student taxes really aren't that hard to understand.
- Student tax software and NETFILE make the whole online thing pretty easy.
- Paying a "seasonal employee" at a big tax-preparation chain to do your return for you is definitely not worth it.
- Being organized makes doing your taxes a lot easier (duh).
- If you don't use up all of your tax credits, they can be carried forward and taken advantage of when you're making the big bucks after you get your degree or diploma.

CHAPTER TEN
BUDGETING BASICS, A.K.A. FUN AND GAMES

WHEN you first got this book, you excitedly flipped straight to this chapter, right? After all, from what we understand, students are notorious for loving to plan things out and watch their cash pile like a hawk.

O.K., so you probably read the word *budget* and instantly associated it with all kinds of lectures from people who are boring and not nearly as cool as your new smartphone app. No one is going to call budgeting the best thing since sliced bread anytime soon, but here is the great part: reading this chapter will allow you to have more fun. This might sound like a trick that only a teacher would use, but we're being honest here! *Budgeting will definitely allow you to have more fun.* (We were going to say "enhance opportunities for amusement, leisure, and recreation", but that seemed decidedly lame and not fun at all.)

How will spending fifteen minutes every month (that works out to about thirty seconds a day) writing down a bunch of bland numbers allow you to have more fun, you might ask? Well, talk to some post-secondary students in the middle of April sometime and see how much fun they're having when their credit cards look as if they have run a marathon, their phones are being turned off because of unpaid bills, their stomachs are rebelling at the site of yet another ramen-noodles “meal”, and they have to beg their parents for loans to get them through until summer. Not the right kind of excitement for you? Then trust us: budgeting might seem boring, but it's also worth it.

For some reason, adults figure that the best strategy for getting students to budget is to tell them in stern voices that, back in their day, they survived on $1.63 a month, that students should live like monks, and that a great budget is one that is painstakingly difficult to make and involves lots of numbers-crunching. Have these people met students lately? Crew, we'll let you in on a little secret: this stuff isn't that hard. We have this little thing called the Internet, which makes budgeting super easy and speedy. Really, all budgeting consists of is making a few decisions about what you really want to do and what you really want to own. Unless you're rich (in which case you probably aren't reading this book), you simply can't do and have everything you want in life (at least not all at once, right now), so budgeting is basically thinking about this for a few minutes and then deciding what really generates the most joy for you in relation to its price. That's it! You pick what you want most, and then ensure that you get it first. Stuff you want least waits until later. Who doesn't want the best stuff first?

Numbers Made Easy

The mechanics of budgeting also aren't as difficult as we stodgy adults make them out to be. To start, we recommend going to *myuniversitymoney.com/my-university-money-interactive-student-budget/* and using the custom student budget template; it will calculate everything for you if you put in just a few numbers. Chances are that your bank or credit union has something similar—but probably not as good as the template we recommend. We often find that the initial reaction when students check out the colour-coded template is surprise at the number of monthly expenses they hadn't thought about. (When you live at home, your parents are great at paying for a lot of this stuff so that you never think about the money it takes.) Students aren't just surprised: often, they're also a little overwhelmed. Take a few breaths: it'll be completely fine. All you have to do is plug in the relevant numbers, and the built-in calculator will take care of the rest. After your first month of doing this, it will get much easier. In fact, if you give it an hour or so at the beginning of the school year, you probably can already make ninety-five percent of your budget for the whole year, because many of the most important costs will already be known. For example, if you know you will be buying a bus pass each month, you can pencil in the cost every month, and the only minor change you might have to worry about would be if the cost went up (usually it will go up only slightly—if at all—during the year). This should allow you to see how much money will have to come out of your account before you add in the other expenses.

Now, in the interests of full disclosure, Justin's going to come clean about something: *I didn't really do an "official budget" for most of the time I was in post-secondary education. I know this is sacrilegious to say in a personal-finance guide, but it is true nonetheless. That being said, there is no doubt I would have been better off if I had done one. One of my main reasons for creating the blog MyUniversityMoney.com, and for writing this book, is to help students have an easier time with stuff I've had to learn the hard way—so do as I say, not as I've done! There are also a few reasons why I got away with not jotting down the exact details of my spending habits. The main reason why I survived this bad habit is that I'm a pretty simple person and I have simple tastes. I also am kind of weird in that I am able to keep a pretty good running tally of my bank balance in my head; and I was oddly adept at planning eight months ahead, compared to the average student. Finally, I had more money (and therefore more of a cushion in case I slipped up) than most students, because of a combination of scholarships, a good summer job, and parental help. But I would recommend that the vast majority of young adults avoid that path. Even if you have a head for a numbers, you should do a formal budget for at least the first few months of the school year. Once you have fully grasped the monthly costs of your education and are familiar with what your income and expenses will be, you might be able to slack a little bit—but there still are undeniable benefits, both short- and long-term, to becoming proficient at this whole budgeting thing.*

There is no one "right" way to budget, but there definitely are plenty of wrong ways. If you think you'll be just fine without jotting some rough numbers down on paper, then consider the following situation that post-secondary students are often in. When you mix young people, who have little experience handling any sort of "real money" at all, with large sums of student loans, RESP money, gifts, scholarships and awards, etc., and then throw them into a world full of retailers who have poured unbelievable mega-bucks into scientifically figuring out the optimal way to separate those young people from that money, guess what happens. It doesn't take an advanced economics degree to figure out that this is a recipe for disaster. Yet, oddly enough, we fail to address this much at all in our formal education system—and many parents have never developed budgeting-skills themselves, never mind thought about passing them on to their children. Really, in a lot of ways, we set up post-secondary students to fail.

A budget really is just *a plan for success*—and there are many different ways of creating and sticking to a budget. Still, you do have to pick one of those ways—because, if you don't have at least some idea of what your dollar figures coming in and going out look like, then you're almost guaranteeing yourself some embarrassing and crappy situations in the near term. Even worse: you could actually be handicapping your adult life for years to come, if you let your anti-budgeting ways go on long enough.

In case those things don't *scare* you into budgeting, here's a little something that just might *entice* you. At Dominican University of California, there's a psychology professor, Gail Matthews, Ph.D. She was curious about a study she'd heard about. In fact, a whole lot of people have heard about the study, which has been mentioned in many books and seminars over the years. Here's how it's usually presented: shortly after graduation, Yale University's class of 1953 was surveyed; the recent grads were asked about their plans for the future; three percent of them had written down their goals and the steps that they would take to reach those goals, while the other ninety-seven percent hadn't; twenty years later, the class of 1953 was surveyed again, and it was found that the three percent who had written down their goals and plans were happier and more content than the other ninety-seven percent—*and* had amassed more wealth than all the ninety-seven percent put together. Astounding and inspiring, right? Actually, it turns out that that popular story is untrue: there was no such survey of Yale's class of 1953 (or Harvard's, as the story sometimes goes). Have we dashed your hopes? Well, Dr. Matthews was curious, and so she did her own study. The subjects were divided into five categories, in terms of how much effort they put into coming up with goals, figuring out what it would take to achieve their goals, and assessing their progress. The people who merely *thought* about their goals turned out to have only little more than *half* the success rate of people who had written down their goals and regularly reviewed their progress toward achieving them. Think about it: the people who did the most goal-related stuff besides just *thinking* about what they wanted to accomplish had almost *twice* the success rate. So now we've debunked a myth—and told you about real scientific evidence that you can get a lot more of what you want from life if you do try *writing down* a plan.

In the case of money (and all the things and experiences it can help you get), the budget is the plan.

Creating a Plan

Alright, enough fear-mongering and enticement. How do you do it? How do you start with a budget for the school year?

Well, even before you look at how much money you are going to make, and where it's going to come from, we would start by simply thinking of a few of life's little luxuries with which you desperately want to reward yourself. For either of us, an example would be an ultra-fast Internet connection. We don't technically need it—but it is something that we both really, really want. What budgeting allows you to do is figure out how you can afford these things that are most important to you. Obviously you have to be realistic, but setting a few carrots at the end of the stick for yourself might give you the motivation you need in order to sit down and have a look at your financial situation.

Next, take the time to find out the actual cost of your monthly expenses. When many students start the budgeting process, there is a temptation to guess (in other words, to use fake, made-up figures), as opposed to taking five minutes to find out how much something really costs. There also can be a strong temptation to round down in order to make the numbers look better—DON'T do this. If you tend to visit the bar scene every week, don't budget $20 a month for booze (unless you're one of those "lucky girls" who always seem to meet "nice guys" who are willing to make your personal-finance situation a little easier by paying many of your costs). If you don't know what the average price of groceries would be for someone of your size and appetite, ask your parents for an estimate. For items such as Internet, insurance, a gym pass, cable, tuition, residence fees, etc., it should be just a matter of finding the monthly figure and plugging it in to the template. For something like a phone bill, average your last six months to estimate your monthly bill for the long term.

Some "experts" will tell you that once your monthly budgeted money for a given category has run out, you should never spend a penny more in that category until next month. We hate the idea of being chained to a budget, and we're fairly certain most students will instantly rebel at this. The solution is fairly simple here. If you have budgeted $150 a month for entertainment, and going to a concert would put you $20 over your budget, simply make sure you spend only $130 the next month. Obviously, one danger here is that people can use this technique to justify "borrowing" from all parts of their budget in order to pay for frivolous things that they don't really need—leading to a shortfall in overall funding and destroying the whole concept of a budget in the first place. Another danger is that, when next month rolls around, habit will get the better of you and you'll still spend $150 (or $170, or maybe even more), and just shove your entertainment budget further and further into the red with each passing month, like those kids always begging their parents for advances on their allowances. So, in our example, let's repeat the simple solution, with a little emphasis: just *make sure* you spend only $130 the next month. A little common sense and planning go a long way. *Your budget is your own flexible plan, which you can adapt at any time as long as the basic principles stay in place.*

Once you have your monthly expenses figured out, jot down some of the one-time costs that you'll probably be stuck with during the upcoming school year. Common items include a new computer or printer, a new pair of basketball shoes, and maybe a real luxury item you want, such as a guitar. To say you're going to go through years of education and never buy yourself a luxury item is a pretty tough row to hoe. Once again, it comes down to deciding what you want most. Some large luxury purchases, such as a car, require a ton of sacrifice—so the corresponding benefit you get from your purchase really ought to match the amount of work you'll have to do to get that item or experience. Setting yourself some enticing goals, such as a trip abroad or another luxury purchase, can truly motivate you to work and push harder than you've been doing.

The key here is balance. You have to prioritize what you really want, because you simply can't have it all at once. (And, besides, many of your wants may change. The desire you felt for a certain toy when you were six has kind of faded now that you're three times as old, hasn't it?) This is where many young students fail in their whole budgeting process. Student loans come in, and large sums of money are sitting in their accounts—or they get a shiny new credit card in the mail—and they don't stop to consider what they *really* want *most* in terms of a "treat" purchase. Instead, many students develop terrible spending habits and never learn how to build for the future: they never learn the concept (let alone the *pleasure*) of delayed gratification. If you're under thirty, you probably don't know what *delayed gratification* means. Pull out your smartphone and Google it, because that is half of this whole personal-finance thing right there, buddy!

Finally, once you have a pretty good idea of your monthly costs and your total costs for a whole year of post-secondary education, you can determine what sort of cash flow you will need for the year and where that money will come from. (We always like to look at yearly as well as monthly costs, because many costs change from year to year.) For some students, this need to cover expenses will lead them to apply for student loans; for others it will result in increased hours at their summer job. Some students want their debt to be at zero when they graduate and simply not owe anyone a cent; others want to be able to travel when they're finished with schooling; and still others don't mind $30,000 in debt if they achieve other goals as they go through their educational journey. We're not saying any of the different preferences is wrong; but it is good to have decided what your goals are and to be aware of your costs, so that you can make educated decisions about the trade-offs necessary to get whatever is most important to you, whether it's debt, an increased workload during the summer or school year, or however else you swing it.

So, back to actually making that budget. Since we're 100-percent sure you have taken all of our advice to heart so far, we'll assume you have had a frank discussion with your parents about how much they plan to help you with your costs while at school. You can pencil this amount in. You can also put in any earnings you can safely count on from summer work (we hope you started looking early and have locked up a good gig!). If this leaves you with a surplus, then congratulations! You are pretty much home free. For most people, the number on the expenses side is bigger than the one on the income side. If you've cut out as many unnecessary expenses as you can bear and your income still isn't enough to cover your costs, then the difference will have to made up through another source of revenue—in other words, another source of money coming into your bank account. The most common option is student loans; other options include scholarships, bursaries, and grants, and part-time work you do while going through school. (There are also options that can get you in real trouble if misused, such as student lines of credit and credit cards.) Coming up with a plan to make up the difference between the money you will have coming in for the year and the money that you plan to spend (preferably with a nice little buffer zone as well) will keep you from having to resort to begging your folks at the last minute (or ignoring large balances on your credit card until you owe a ton of money in interest and fees or, even worse, you get a letter telling you to appear in court).

Once you begin to learn that the less money you spend on the stuff you *have* to buy, the more you can spend on the stuff really *want* to buy, you will probably see for yourself where you can cut costs a little bit. There are countless websites out there (including those of yours truly) that offer cost-cutting tips and strategies, such as buying groceries in bulk, splitting the rent among roommates, and figuring out when the cheap night at the movies is. There are people out there who are absolutely obsessed with cutting budgets to the bone and, while we certainly don't embody that level of commitment, each of us will definitely steal a tip from them here and there if it can save us some hard-earned cash without sacrificing something that brings us a lot of happiness. One trick we've used fairly extensively when it comes to saving money is to think of a big, long-term goal, such as a trip or a vehicle, and then compare each tempting purchase to that goal. Do you want that purchase more than you want your long-term goal? What are you going to remember more fondly five years from now—that trip to the Caribbean, or the fact that you spent $5 on coffee every morning for a year (that's more than

$1,800!)? If you'd rather achieve the big goal, put the small temptation down and walk away. This helps us steer clear of impulse buys and see through advertisers' bags of tricks.

O.K., SO THIS PART ISN'T THAT FUN

Students as a group are really great at burning through money. Often it's not the "big" expenditures that sink us, but rather the day-to-day money that seems to float away without our noticing. In our experience, this pocket money is often gobbled up by a few major "budget-busting" items. Most students we know spend a *ton* of money on the coffee we just mentioned, *and* on eating out, *and* on alcohol. Now, hey, we're not here to preach at you (O.K., maybe a little): if you honestly get a *ton* of enjoyment from those three things, then they could very well be worth the bite they take out of your budget: for most students, however, we think the relatively low price *per item* distracts them from the *overall* blow to their budget that these items collectively strike.

One activity that a lot of the "gurus" out there recommend doing is tracking all of your expenses for a week or, even better, for a month. If this seems familiar to you, chances are you have talked to a nutritionist before! The principle behind writing down every nickel that you spend and every single morsel of food you put in your mouth is the same: you will probably be shocked when you add it all up. It's so easy to justify spending a little bit of money at a time that it probably snowballs much faster than you would think.

There is a guy who writes about personal finance for a living named David Bach, and he has basically made his name on the idea of "The Latte Factor". His premise is that, if you spend what seems like "a little" every day on things like coffee (especially the pricey, frou-frou kind), you are wasting a fortune (yes, an actual fortune) over the course of your life. His idea is that, if you invest that $2.00 a day (or however much your coffee is), you can be a *millionaire* on *that money alone* when you're ready to retire. Now, in our experience, most students can have a hard time seeing past next Saturday night, let alone to a time when their own kids will be off at college—so this line of thinking doesn't really enter into their quest for immediate gratification. But that doesn't change the fact that a cup of coffee for 100 days each semester can *seriously* set you back and you probably won't even realize it. Going out to eat should be a treat, *not* the norm. So just watch for these sneaky little costs: they can rapidly undo all the good work you've put into keeping your head above water financially.

In the end, budgeting is just about having a plan. Who doesn't like having a plan to get a ton of cool stuff from life? Chances are that you are entering the first period of your life in which you have actual control over relatively large sums of money. If you have no plan to compensate for your lack of experience with having control over that much money, bad things are likely to happen. If you use one of the zillion budgeting apps that are available to help you, check out our free budgeting template online, and use a little common sense when thinking about what you should be spending money on, you'll be just fine. And, hey, at the end of the day, if you stick to ninety percent of your budgeting plans and goals, you're doing better than most "adults" in the world today, not to mention our government—so cheers!

Chapter 10 Summary

- Budgeting isn't as hard or painful as people make it out to be. Check out our user-friendly budget template: myuniversitymoney.com/my-university-money-interactive-student-budget/
- Budgets allow you to make sure you get the most fun possible out of your scrawny student bank account.
- Small everyday purchases like coffee or cigarettes can sink your budget in a hurry!

CHAPTER ELEVEN

"DUDE, WHERE'S MY CAR?"

WHO doesn't want to own a car? I know there are some of you who are better than we are and have morals that revolve around little things like saving our environment. Most of us, however, have been fully corrupted by the North American car culture. We don't want to take the blue pill and wake up to the fact that we are pouring money down the drain and doing a good deal of damage to the life on our planet in the process. (Sorry: the "blue pill" reference comes from a movie that most of you have probably never seen, called *The Matrix*. At one time it was considered ground-breaking and there was a video game for it and everything. Yes, Keanu Reeves was ground-breaking at one time—and, yeah, we were there and that still sounds weird.) The truth is that owning a car is an absolute money pit. Almost every piece of literature we've read on building wealth says not to spend money on vehicles, because they are heavily depreciating assets that cost a ton to own. This means not only that you pay something to keep the car on the road, but also that the whole time you own the car it is becoming worth less and less money.

Kyle's confession time: *I was pretty aware of the whole money-pit thing even as a young adult, and yet I still decided to own a vehicle while I went through school. In an effort to defend myself, I will say that*

*Winnipeg's public-transit system *cough, cough* leaves much to be desired, and that as a rural kid I found the car very useful in order to get home on the odd weekend. In my situation, I weighed the costs of owning a car and the sacrifices I would have to make in order to do it, against the benefits it provided me. Becoming a part of the infrastructure problem in North America was the choice I made. Looking back on it, I'm not sure what I would do if I could do it over again, but there is no doubt that it did cost me a ton of money. The car I owned while going to school was a 2002 Pontiac Grand Prix, which I bought after my second year, in 2007. I had gotten quite a few awards and scholarships in my first year of school, and I had lived very frugally, so, with a little help from my folks, I purchased the vehicle that summer without any loan at all. I can definitely see how I was influenced as much by the social status of having a car as I was by the utility of it. But the fact is that not having a vehicle is probably a much smarter decision for many students across Canada.*

For our parents' generation, car ownership was almost a given, especially for men. Today, however, there are plenty of public-transit options that are becoming better and better across the Great White North, and there is also considerable incentive to choose these options. Using a public-transit pass isn't the only option besides owning a vehicle. More and more people in urban environments are bucking the sedentary-lifestyle trend that has been killing our hearts and expanding our waistlines over the past few decades. Biking, walking, or jogging to school periodically, while using a public-transit pass as a backup, is a great way to save on gym costs while staying in shape and using solid time-management principles. Eating a little more in the way of healthful food to fuel your body will definitely cost less than the oil they're pumping out of the ground in the Middle East.

PRIVATE VS. PUBLIC TRANSPORTATION

The problem with making blanket statements about what mode of transportation to recommend across Canada is the incredible variety of climates and public-transit options and their price points. Standing in line for a bus in February in Winnipeg or Edmonton is not remotely the same as in Vancouver or Toronto. Sometimes those −40° mornings make owning a vehicle look pretty attractive; this was especially true when Winnipeg's public-transit system was so lacklustre (we'll try not to tangent too badly here). Likewise, in rural and semi-rural areas, commuting by personal vehicle is not considered optional. This is something to consider if you're comparing living on campus with commuting from home. There is no doubt that the government is trying to encourage students (and everyone else) to use public transit: after all, they created the public-transit tax credit in 2007. The Yukon Territory has a similar tax credit, but no other provinces or territories did as of 2012, according to the Canada Revenue Agency. This is a nice little carrot on the stick and further widens the cost gap between owning a personal vehicle and having a public-transit pass. Finally, when you buy a public-transit pass, there are very few hidden costs. The rate is public, and it isn't as if the service will suddenly disappear or charge you for repairs.

On some post-secondary campuses across Canada, student unions have decided to make an even stronger case for public transit. In what is usually a fairly controversial conversation across our campuses, some student populations have voted in favour of simply including the costs for public-transit passes in the tuition fees charged to every student. In most cases, this fee is automatic and non-refundable. When students vote to buy in mass like this, it drives down the cost of an individual public-transit pass for each student; however, it also forces students who prefer personal vehicles to subsidize (pay for) those who use nothing but public transit. If it is already included in your fees, it may really be in your best interest to figure out a way to make public transit work in your favour. The financial benefits tend to slant the table pretty fast. Take a look at your tuition breakdown in your student financial account at your school's website to see whether the fee has been charged and is mandatory, or simply ask at the Registrar's Office.

We have to admit that our experience with Winnipeg's public-transit system sort of jaded us to the idea in and of itself. Students' constant frustration with the lack of a rapid-transit option and with any sort of reliability in the winter has been going on for some time now. Some of the packages offered across the rest of the country seem a lot more valuable and useful. Vancouver, for example, offers a universal pass (U-Pass), which gives post-secondary students access not only to the bus network, but also to the SeaBus and SkyTrain services—all for the low price of $30 a month, averaging just under $1 a day. Combined with the more hospitable weather, it's definitely an attractive option. By comparison, Winnipeg charges more than $60 a month for its patchwork bus network. Other recent post-secondary monthly pass rates grabbed quickly from the Web range from $44 in Montreal for a combined Metro and bus pass, to $75 for a student bus pass in Saskatoon and $77 in Edmonton, all the way up to a $104 subway pass in Toronto. Regardless of the specific cost for your student public-transit pass, one thing is certain: it's going to cost you less than a personal vehicle will.

THE TRUE COST OF A CAR

If you're like us and just assumed while growing up that everyone had a vehicle, you'll probably be shocked to find out the true cost involved with the cult of vehicle ownership. We had never really considered this before we started doing a lot of reading in the personal-finance world, and by that time we had already been driving cars that we owned for a couple years!

The upfront cost of a vehicle is its purchase price—which is relatively straightforward. Usually, the first two things students decide when shopping for cars are what kind they want and whether to buy new or used. Almost all of the students we know need only the basic transportation provided by a used car; however, some do get sucked in to buying new. If you choose to buy new and to "finance" the vehicle (that's salesman speak for borrowing money for a car you can't yet afford), you have to include the considerable interest charges you will pay through financing. (Remember, interest is the money you have to pay the bank for the service of lending you the money.) The special finance offers you see in advertisements are for people with great credit scores—not young students. You will be paying a premium for the loan, which means large interest payments. Take the huge amount of money needed to buy a car in the first place, add the interest for borrowing money to buy something you don't already have the money for, and what you get is a monthly payment toward that loan that gobbles up a gigantic part of your budget. We could go into more detail but, for now, our strong advice is not to get into "financing" a car if you're a student.

It's interesting to us that people rationalize buying a car because they believe it will mean they own something that's worth what they just paid for it. Automobiles are not like a house or land, however: they depreciate (lose their monetary value) quickly. Various estimates put the average depreciation of a car at ten to twenty percent per year, depending on the make and model. For those of you who aren't math whizzes, let's look at a few scenarios. First, let's say you spend $10,000 on a used car that's a few years old, and that the car is made by a well respected company that has a solid reputation in the used-car market and consequently the vehicle depreciates just ten percent a year. After you've owned it for one year, the car's resale value (what you could get for it if you sold it) would be $9,000. Two years down the road, the value would be $8,100. At three years, the car would be worth $7,290; at four years, $6,561. After five years, that car you bought for $10,000 would be worth about $5,905. Alternatively, if you purchased a used car for the same $10,000, and the used-car market decides that it isn't a well made vehicle and you're looking at twenty-percent depreciation a year, and then the values would look like this: $8,000 after year one, $6,400 after year two, $5,120 after year three, $4,096 after year four, and *just $3,277* after five years.

The loss of value for a used car looks bad . . . until you compare it to the depreciation of a new model. Let's look at what would happen if you purchased a new car for $20,000 and watched it depreciate twenty percent per year. The almost new car would fetch $16,000 after one year of use, $12,800 after two years, $10,240 after three years, and $8,192 after four years; just five years after buying your shiny new car, you now can get about $6,554 for it. That is $13,446 of value that you have "used up" or watched evaporate in five years! When you compare that to the earlier example of depreciation in a used car (a loss over five years of about $4,100 to about $6,700), you can see why a new car is considered an expensive luxury and a terrible investment by most financially savvy thinkers out there. Depreciation is part of the true cost of owning a vehicle, because it is effectively money that has left your pocket as you've owned the car. Of course, you can limit the number of dollars lost to depreciation if you buy an older vehicle that has already lost most of its original value. Older cars do tend to chew into your budget in other ways, though.

The next big hit is yearly repairs and maintenance. The simple rule of thumb is that the more maintenance you do, the fewer repairs you have to take care of, so we recommend taking an hour to read the owner's manual so you know when your car should have fluid changes and the like. Most people usually do three oil changes in a year, which costs roughly $150 if you don't do it yourself, in addition to other periodic maintenance. No matter how much maintenance you do, some repairs are always necessary, including the basic changing of tires, brake pads, alternator, battery, etc. The cost of repairs varies widely, depending on the make and model of your car; a hopeful estimate puts the cost for most used vehicles at $1,000 a year.

Insurance companies are not big fans of the under-25 crowd. Before you get mad at them, consider how much more often you and your buddies, or other people your age, do dumb things in vehicles, compared to your parents. That's why you have to pay a lot more to get insured than they do. Our insurance in Manitoba was about $120 a month when we were starting university back in 2005 (about $1,400 a year!), and that is among the cheapest you'll find in Canada.

If you're at fault in an accident that damages your car, your insurance won't cover all the costs of repairs, for there's also the matter of the **deductible**, which is the part you pay from your own pocket for the repair costs before the insurance kicks in to cover the rest. You can get a policy in which the deductible is relatively small (a few hundred dollars); but you'll pay a higher monthly price (also called the **premium**) for that policy. Or you can reduce your monthly premium by getting a policy with a higher deductible; but then you'd better have money in savings, because if the mechanic needs $1,200 to do the repair and the first $1,000 of that price is your responsibility (the deductible) then you won't be going anywhere until you fork it over. In addition, if you were indeed the cause of the accident, your insurance company will find out, will conclude that insuring you is a bigger risk, and will start charging you a higher price for insurance.

Electric cars might be the way of the future, but they're not here yet (at least not as far as a student budget is concerned). That means gasoline prices must be part of your analysis. If you fill your tank twice a month, you're looking at a minimum of $100. A much likelier figure is $150, and many students easily spend $200 or more per month on gas. *This alone costs more than your public-transit pass.*

Finally, we get to every student's favourite subject—parking. Parking rates obviously differ across Canada. At the University of Manitoba, it cost about $500 to get a residence parking-spot for eight months. Parking at most apartments costs somewhat less than that, but not *much* less. Then you have to consider the times when you will park off campus. In Winnipeg, you can get away with usually finding relatively cheap parking; but, in many places, this is not an option. You could probably throw in at least another $200 per year in most cities for random parking costs. The University of Manitoba is a conservative example; parking near many university campuses is much pricier than that.

A cost we won't bother to put a number on, but one that affects many students, is parking-tickets and speeding-tickets. You all know the drill: a group meeting runs late and you don't get to the meter; you miss your alarm for your final exam and are trying to make up time; etc. These tickets can range from a minor annoyance to a week's worth of part-time wages. And, while the only cost of parking-tickets is the ticket's face value and the inconvenience of paying it, speeding-tickets are another story: the police report your "moving-violations" (laws you break while your car is in motion) to your insurance company—and the company rightly interprets this as evidence that you're a riskier driver and starts charging you more money for insurance.

By our count, once you add up all of these costs, you're looking at a true vehicle cost of about $5,000 a year, in addition to the depreciation of the car. This value is Manitoba-based. If your province charges higher insurance rates—or if you live in a big city, such as Vancouver or Toronto, and have to deal with higher parking fees—you could be looking at a much greater cost. For those of you keeping score at home, this means that the financial sacrifice for the convenience of having a car while you go to school is pretty much at least $4,000 a year (the difference between your car and the price of a public-transit pass)—and it could reach a lot higher than that. Plus there is the original price you paid for the vehicle itself. One other consideration for students: your vehicle is an asset that has to be declared on student-loan forms, and it does reduce the amount of money you can get (and can even keep you from getting any student loans at all).

DEVIL'S ADVOCATE

Now we would be remiss if we didn't quickly mention the benefits of having your own ride. Probably the biggest reasons to get your own car are the time saved and the convenience factor. For example, Kyle is obsessive about not waiting in line for things and trying to make efficient use of time, so this played a huge role in his choice to have his own vehicle. The ability to control your own fate (at least transportation-wise) regardless of public holidays, the hour of the day or night, bad weather, labour strikes, or any other such factor can be addictive. If you're commuting from a rural area or bedroom community, there is basically no choice in the matter: you obviously need a car.

The biggest reason for many of us to get a car is that our present culture has decreed it to be just plain cool. Whether anyone wants to admit it or not, there is still a little smidge of a stigma about taking the bus for a date—although we believe this is quickly disappearing, because of that whole "we are destroying our environment" thing that everyone's talking about these days. Still, as long as rock and rap music videos keep showing "pimped-out rides", there will be a demand for them.

So where does this leave you? Cars might be great for dates, but actually having the money to go on dates is a pretty sweet deal too. We know many students who live at home while going to school and who do the public-transit thing but are able to borrow their parents' rides liberally much of the time. Obviously, if you have accommodating parents, this is a great option. For rural kids living close to campus or in residence, one option for your old high-school car that's falling apart is to keep it at home during the school year and then just register it and drive it when you're home for the summer. If public transit isn't your thing, but a car just seems out of your reach, consider bugging your friends to carpool with them regularly. If you are going to do this, don't be cheap! Pay up for gas, now that you know how much it's costing your buddy to drive your educated butt around!

Basically, if you're serious about building wealth from a young age, then owning a car is a huge handicap. If the sacrifice is worth it you *and* you can fit it in your budget, owning a car might be O.K. in your specific situation. We would never advise a student to take on debt in order to own a car. If you can't afford to pay it down in cash, then in our opinion owning a vehicle probably isn't your best option. You can always use it as a carrot on a stick in order to motivate yourself to work a second job in the summer or something like that, but using your student loan to buy a car is probably not justifiable under any circumstance.

Automobile Associations

We've saved the upbeat news for last. Auto clubs or associations are about big savings for everyone in three groups: those of you who own your own cars; those of you who occasionally (or even more frequently) drive someone else's car (whether borrowed or rented); and even those of you who don't drive at all. These are organizations that focus on helping people who drive cars, but some of them offer big benefits that stretch into many other parts of your financial life. By far the biggest, best-known one in Canada is the Canadian Automobile Association (CAA), with close to six million members and 140 offices across the country.

For about 18¢ to 38¢ a day, depending on the membership level you choose, you get serious coverage for your butt in those annoying circumstance almost every driver (or passenger) gets into at one point or another—locking the keys inside, needing a jump-start, running out of fuel, needing a tow truck, etc. Those are the main benefits many people think of when they consider CAA. But, more often, CAA members take advantage of all kinds of other offerings, which you can learn more about at *CAA.ca*. Basically, your membership card will get you upfront discounts on all sorts of products and services, such as gas, hotels and motels, and car rentals. In addition, when you present your card at certain retailers, you earn CAA dollars, which can be used to reduce or eliminate your already cheap annual membership renewal fee.

Many parents choose to start their kids with a membership that's part of the household membership. This saves money—and gives parents a lot of peace of mind as their little darlings leave home in their shiny cars. Kyle's mom purchased his membership as his birthday present every year on the family's plan as he went through school, and he eventually switched to his own separate membership when he was finally told it was time to grow up. So far, he's been fortunate enough not to need the free towing; but, more than once, a friendly CAA employee has solved locked-keys and dead-battery dilemmas. Just one call from the free locksmith probably saved more money than a whole year's membership costs.

Chapter 11 Summary

- Motor vehicles are depreciating assets.
- There are many hidden costs to consider when you're buying a vehicle, such as insurance, maintenance, repairs, gas, and parking fees.
- Public transportation might not win you many status points, but it's definitely cheaper.
- The true cost of owning a car is roughly $5,000 per year (in addition to what it costs to buy it), and your insurance costs could raise that figure substantially.
- No one makes action movies about dudes who take the bus . . . so we guess car owners have that.

CHAPTER TWELVE

CREDIT CARDS AND LINES OF CREDIT

IF you have ever been to a post-secondary campus during the first two weeks of the fall semester, you've probably noticed the attractive displays and booths set up by credit-card distributors. Credit-card companies make oodles of money, and they can afford to hire some pretty smart people in their marketing departments. This usually results in clever little giveaways and freebies that entice impressionable young students into signing up for their product. A 2009 study found that nine out of ten graduating university students now had at least one credit card each. Yet some financial "gurus" tell young people to avoid credit cards at all costs: "They're evil!" they shout from their mountaintops of frugality.

We don't belong in that group of "experts". Much like any other tool, a credit card has perfectly valid uses and can fill a variety of needs for a student. At the same time, abusing a credit card can absolutely wreck your finances for many, many years to come. Credit cards are not the root of all financial evil, but financial illiteracy is—and the two put together can be disastrous.

To understand fully just how credit cards can throw you off your game so quickly, it is kind of important to understand how interest, especially compound interest, works. Yes, there is some math involved here, but don't worry—we're not math guys either, so we'll keep it simple. Before we look at any numbers, it's worth taking a peak at what a wise man once said about compound interest:

"The most powerful force in the universe is compound interest."

The great thing about compound interest is that, when you start to invest, it's going to work in your favour and it will help make many of you millionaires. (Because you're going to graduate debt-free after reading this book, you'll be on the right track.) The other side of the same coin is that compound interest is just as powerful when it works against you—which is what it does when you borrow money—and it creates a negative feedback cycle that can quickly drown you in debt.

BE AFRAID . . . BE VERY AFRAID

Just so the powers that be are satisfied, we'll illustrate the worst-case scenario that can result from irresponsible credit-card use, before we let you in on why you should get one anyway. When you borrow money on a credit card, the credit-card company charges you interest on the amount of money that you borrowed. (The amount you initially borrow is called the **principal**. For a refresher on the basic concept of interest, turn to page 69 and to the GLOSSARY.) Let's look at an example, and for this you'll need to know that when you "carry a balance" you're paying back less than the full amount you owe—each month, some money you borrowed more than a month ago still hasn't been paid back. If your credit card has an annual interest rate of 19.99 percent, and you carry a balance of $100 all year while paying back only the interest each month, you will have paid the credit card company roughly $20 in interest by the end of the year—on top of the original $100 you borrowed. When you use small amounts, like that $100, this doesn't seem so bad—but this can snowball in a hurry. Carrying $1,000 for the year will cost you *$200*—and we've seen a few students graduate with $5,000 or more in credit-card debt, and *it was costing them $1,000 and up, every year,* *just to pay the interest!* Even worse problems arise when you can't even pay all your *interest* every month, let alone any of the principal. Most credit cards will let you pay a small monthly minimum payment, usually $10 or about three percent of your balance, whichever one is larger. What happens at this point is that, if you can't afford to pay back at least your interest, it gets tacked on to the principal you already owed and essentially becomes part of a newer, and larger, principal. This doesn't just happen at the end of the year: it happens every month—when next month comes, the new interest you owed this month will be considered just the same as the original amount you borrowed, and they'll charge you interest *on the interest too*. That is what they call **compound interest**, and it can sink you quickly. You're paying for the privilege of borrowing money to pay for the privilege of borrowing money, to pay for the privilege of . . . you see the pattern—and it goes back as many months (or years) as it's been since you first swiped your card to buy something, and lasts until you've finally paid every penny you owe, including all the interest, and get things back down to zero.

This negative example of compound interest is one reason why Rule Number One of most personal-finance gurus is to pay off your credit-card balance every month. Indeed, although we each use our credit cards to the tune of several hundred dollars a month, we always pay the full balance. Credit-card companies hate people like us, the ones who pay their balances monthly: we get all the advantages of credit-card use without paying any interest (and interest is the main way the credit-card banks make their money).

So, who would be crazy enough to carry a balance on a credit card, you might ask? Well, according to a report released in 2011 by TD Bank, twenty-one percent of Canadians made *only* the *minimum* required payments on their credit cards. And, according to a Prairie Research Associates study from 2009, twenty-four percent of graduating Canadian university students reported carrying an average monthly balance of $3,440. It's probably safe to say that most of those students would not have felt comfortable walking around every month thinking "I owe my friend more than three thousand bucks—and I owed her three thousand last month, and the month before, and the month before that." But the credit-card banks don't have a personal relationship with you: they just send you a bit of paper every month, and they "kindly" tell you that this month you need to pay them not even one twentieth of the full amount you owe them—and, even though you owe them so much, they won't mind at all if you borrow some more to pay for that night on the town you so desperately "need". To put it mildly, this setup is not good news.

Here is a little frame of reference for you, as far as how interest rates work in the financial world and how quickly credit cards can mess up your life. Wall Street sharks are generally hailed as geniuses if they can turn $100 into $112 or $115 over the course of a year and maintain that rate of growth for a good while (and that's before fees and taxes chip away at the growth). That's just 12 to 15 percent we're talking about. You can beat the sharpest minds on Wall Street by simply paying off your credit card with its 19.99-percent annual interest rate, because that is nearly a *20-percent* return and it's *after* taxes are taken into consideration!

This is worth repeating: DO NOT carry a monthly balance on your credit card if you can at all help it! And, if you carry it one month, do everything you can do to get rid of it the next month.

CREDIT CARDS DON'T KILL BANK ACCOUNTS—PEOPLE DO

There. Now that we've covered the personal-finance basics, let's take a look at why you should ignore those gurus who think you can't handle a little piece of plastic in your wallet.

The best reason to get a credit card while you're in school is that responsibly using one will help build your credit rating. Once you graduate and set out to buy a car or a house, this little thing called a **credit score** will start to creep in to your life. A credit rating, as it's also called, is a three-digit number that summarizes your credit report. Your **credit report** is basically your report card on how well you've handled credit; it traces your history over several years, including all the ups and downs. If you've never paid a monthly bill, never opened a line of credit, and never borrowed money from any institution, your credit score will actually be worse than those of people who are in a little bit of debt but have proved themselves able to make consistent payments to get rid of the debt. This might sound strange—that a person who owes money has an easier time borrowing more money than someone who owes no money at all—but it is true nonetheless. Having a student credit card, using it rarely, and always paying off the monthly balance are a great way to show that you are responsible with credit.

If worse comes to worst, always remember that you absolutely **HAVE** to make the *minimum required* payment on any debt that you have. If you fail to make a minimum payment, you will probably default on the debt, and your credit score could be badly hurt. Rebuilding it will take years; and, while we're sure your credit score means less than the score in the hockey game last night when you're eighteen, trust us—it will matter a whole lot more in a few years. If you ever want to be able to borrow money in your life (and you're extremely unlikely ever to be able to own a home without borrowing), it's worth taking into consideration.

When you're searching for a student credit card that's right for you, it's probably simplest to take a look at the offering of whatever bank you have a student bank account with. (If you don't even have a bank account—get one. Compared to conducting your financial life with cash and gift cards, banking saves you a ton of time, a ton of effort, and even a ton of money. It's also much safer, drastically reducing the risk that your money will disappear without your intending it.) A decent student credit card will have no annual fee (you shouldn't pay just for having a card, but some banks do charge exactly that kind of fee) and an interest rate under twenty percent (get it as low as you can find, just in case there is a month when you don't pay your entire balance). Some student cards today even have small rewards programs, which give you a little money back, collect air miles for you, or even reward you with free tickets to movies. As long as the card doesn't have an annual fee and has a low interest rate, feel free to choose whatever rewards program fits you best.

What factors should *not* affect your choice of card? The fact that it is (or isn't) decorated with a cool picture or the logo of your favourite hockey team. Also, don't pick a particular card just because its marketers had the best giveaway the first week of school: the free team blanket or school T-shirt is the oldest trick in the book.

Take a quick look at the information pamphlet to see whether the student card meets our qualifications before signing on any dotted line! In the ideal world, a student credit card will make your life easier (online shopping, anyone?), allow you to build a credit rating, get you some cool rewards, and never cost you a nickel.

Finally, one last time, repeat after us: "I . . . will . . . NOT . . . carry a balance on my credit card!"

STUDENT LINES OF CREDIT

Since you're now all experts on that whole pesky credit-card thing and can avoid every doomsday scenario, let's take a look at the other main credit option available to students.

If you're set up with a bank or credit union under a student plan, chances are you have received promotional materials for their student lines of credit (SLOCs). Like credit cards, SLOCs can be beneficial if used properly—and can really get a student behind the debt 8-ball if they're used just to pursue "the moment" with no thought for the future. A SLOC really isn't that different in most ways from a regular line of credit, and is not in any way a student loan. Unlike a student loan, a SLOC can be used for anything a student wants: it's basically a running balance with a limit. The limits for most undergraduate student lines of credit are between $5,000 and $10,000.

Both of us had SLOCs when in school, but with limits under $5,000. The interest rate on a SLOC usually ranges from prime plus one percent to prime plus three percent, and then floats up and down with the bank's prime rate. Take a look at our sections on repaying student loans, starting on page 79, for an explanation of interest rates, what "prime" is, and why that stuff is important. Most institutions allow students to make interest-only payments on their SLOCs until they graduate.

A student line of credit is sort of a midpoint between a student loan and carrying a credit-card balance. Student loans are really a much better option, because they do not accumulate interest until after you've finished school; even when you've finished your studies, the student loan is better because the interest on it is tax-deductible, whereas the interest on your SLOC is not. While interest-only payments on SLOCs might sound attractive at first (they usually keep the monthly costs pretty manageable), paying just the interest is not a good cycle to get into. Undergraduates carrying thousands of dollars on a SLOC, month after month, are probably locked in to bad spending habits. But SLOCs are a much better option than carrying a balance on a student credit card. As we just talked about, carrying a balance on a credit card sucks in so many ways. The difference between interest-rates on a SLOC and on a credit card is huge. Right now, the interest rate is prime plus one percent on some of the student lines of credit available at the major banks. Our current prime lending rate is three percent, so, at the moment, the effective rate of interest is four percent on a SLOC from RBC, for example. We don't think the Bank of Canada will raise interest rates much—but, next year, prime could conceivably be 4.5 percent or 5 percent. That's still a much better deal than your student credit card can offer. We're big fans of using a credit card for their convenience, to track spending, to get rewards, and to build a credit rating; but carrying a balance on it should be a last resort. Using any space left on your SLOC to pay off your credit-card balance is probably a good idea—as long as you are not addicted to debt and you don't just go refill your credit card to the max again!

SLOCS FOR GRADUATE STUDENTS AND DENTISTS

It is worth noting that there are much different rules and expectations for SLOCs when you are a graduate student, specifically if you're going into certain professions, such as medicine and dentistry, that have high tuition costs but also have high expected future earnings. Most graduate-student limits range from $40,000 to $50,000, with yearly limits as well. Dental students, who have to pay for many of their tools up front in addition to high tuition rates, can usually sign on the dotted line to access up to $200,000 from a SLOC. Those studying to be lawyers, doctors, pharmacists, and optometrists also have access to much bigger loans, including all the opportunities for success (and financial nightmares) that come with such big loans. In addition to having access to higher-paying jobs (and a corresponding higher probability of paying off large loans), these future professionals are very valuable long-term consumers to banks. Think about the profits that are waiting to be made from someone who earns a $200,000 yearly salary. Such a person's investment portfolio alone probably generates massive profits for a bank, and such persons are likelier than others to take out large mortgages and conduct other big transactions with the bank. The brand loyalty that can be established early in a professional's life is worth hundreds of thousands of dollars, which is another reason why banks are willing to lend so much to students going into those fields. The value of brand loyalty also is important to remember if you're negotiating an interest rate and you're in this enviable career position.

A GOOD TOOL IN YOUR TOOL BELT

There is little doubt that many students abuse lines of credit and student credit cards, and that access to credit of any kind can and does hurt a large portion of Canadian students. That being said, we believe that almost all students should have both credit options set up, for two main reasons. The first is to help with emergencies, when there may be a quick need for a few thousand bucks (such as when you're a commuter and your engine blows). The second reason is that student lines of credit and student credit cards are great methods for establishing a solid credit rating. Just remember to remind your less responsible friends that a student line of credit is not actually code for "Shots, shots, shots . . . EVERYBODY."

Chapter 12 Summary

- Credit cards are not inherently bad. They are a tool that should be used properly but often isn't.
- Carrying a balance on a credit card is the first thing you should do if your goal is to become familiar with bankruptcy legislation.
- Some student credit cards offer cool points and rewards programs, but the most important factors should be a low interest rate and no fees.
- Student lines of credit can be a great alternative to credit cards, but they are definitely not equivalent to student loans.

CHAPTER THIRTEEN
TEN WAYS AROUND THE TEXTBOOK BLACK HOLE

ONE major hidden expense of going to university is paying for textbooks. Most people don't realize that a full course load's worth of brand new textbooks from the school bookstore can easily run over a thousand dollars for two semesters! It doesn't appear that prices will come down soon either, because the cost of textbooks is increasing at a rate four times that of general inflation. The good news is that there are lots of ways to bring this number down to something more reasonable. Whatever you do, DO NOT go straight to your campus bookstore and buy a brand-new copy of everything on your book list.

1. Go to the First Class First

Often, professors have to hand in their book lists for the fall semester at the end of the winter semester. This means that they often don't really care what they write down and it's the last thing on their minds as they're getting final grades out and deciding which tropical destinations to go to for their breaks. The result is that professors throw down the names of all of the books they might want use in the course—but, when you show up the first day, each professor probably will say, "This is the main textbook for the course, and these other ones make great supplemental reading." This is code for "You really need only this one book, but if you want to go from an *A* to an *A*+ you could probably read these . . . oh, yeah, and this one I actually wrote myself, which is the only reason it's on the list."

2. Never Buy Your Books from the Campus Bookstore!

We're closet book nerds, so campus bookstores are feel-good places for us. They have all this great knowledge packaged in shiny new vessels. It makes you feel like a real part of higher learning. Feel free to soak up the atmosphere and even throw in a job application there—but, if you want to save your money, don't buy your textbooks there! If you check regularly, the bookstore will often have some good deals on school-branded clothing and other assorted items, but textbooks never go on sale. People running the store realize that most students will blindly walk in with book lists and assume that this is the only real option to buy their textbooks. If that's your assumption too, they have you in their trap. What's so bad about this trap? Campus bookstores' prices are way higher than you'd pay elsewhere for the same books.

3. Buy from Other Students

Why line the pockets of the huge companies that change editions constantly and care only for profit margins? Buy from your fellow students and save your money! In our experience, students will usually give you a fair price for your book and ask for a fair price in return if the book is in decent shape. At the University of Manitoba, we had a used-bookstore run by the student union. We thought it was a brilliant business model. You set your own price on the book you wanted to sell (usually after looking at similar copies already on the shelves) and then the administration kept track of everything else. There was even an automatic-deposit option, whereby your earnings were deposited into your bank account without any ongoing effort on your part. In return for the services offered, the store took as profit a relatively small percentage of the price each book sold for. This plan works especially well for large first-year classes.

4. Buy Online

Amazon.ca, *Amazon.com*, *AddAll.com*, *BigWords.com*, *BookFinder.com*, *DealOz.com*, and numerous other websites (just Google "buy textbooks online") offer very competitive prices, and many make comparison shopping a breeze. The only caution we would give when you're ordering online is to remember to include the cost of shipping—and remember that, for many vendors, sending books to Canada requires international shipping. On the other hand, if you do a quick search for online coupons or promotional codes, you can often take off another ten to thirty percent with two minutes' work. We usually aren't self-disciplined enough to use coupons, but even we can handle a quick Google search if it'll save us some hard-earned cash.

5. If You Live in Residence, Try Putting Up a Poster

One of the many benefits of living in residence and being around hundreds of other students is that there is a ready-made market for used textbooks. This is especially true because so many residence students are in their first year and therefore in many of the same classes. Every year, we sold and bought books by simply putting up a few posters in high-traffic areas, such as the elevator and lounges, with our names and room numbers attached. There were always lots of books for *fifty percent* off the cover price, and all you had to do was walk down the hall to take advantage of the savings.

6. Buy Older Editions if You Can Get Away with It

No matter whether your textbook was published in 2006 or 2009, Julius Cæsar still died on the Ides of March, adding the squares of the two sides will still equal the square of the hypotenuse of a right triangle, and E still equals mc^2. In many fields, not much changes in new editions of textbooks, except an introduction and an appendix or two. If you want to pay top dollar for this appendix, that's up to you; but major bucks can be saved by purchasing last year's edition. Most students simply look at their book lists and don't stray very far. This means that there's little demand for the old edition—and guess what that means for your lucky capitalistic self. Low demand means low price. Low price means more money for important stuff, like drink specials.

7. Some Books You Can Completely Download Free

There are cases where entire books can be downloaded at no cost whatsoever—especially if you're an English major. Copyright laws state that many older works are no longer protected, so they are free to be downloaded and copied by anyone. Check out *Gutenberg.org* for more details. Basically, that anthology of a hundred old poems that was going to cost you $100, and which your professor was going to assign four pages of, is now free.

8. Often, the Professor Puts a Few Copies of the Book in the Library

If you are especially committed to saving your money, you might try perusing a textbook at the library whenever you need it. Usually your professor will have a copy or two on reserve. This may be annoying, because it forces you to do all your reading at the library and the book often is signed out when you get there; but, if it is one of those classes where only a few chapters of reading are needed, it sure beats paying $100!

9. Sell Them Back . . . Just Not to the Bookstore

If you know any older students, they probably have stacks of old textbooks sitting in their basements, collecting dust. The only fringe benefit we've seen from these books is that when they are on view they can act as a sort of chest-puffing display for academic types. This is not our style, so we would recommend selling the books. Chances are you'll see all kinds of advertisements encouraging you to sell your textbooks back to the bookstore. Most bookstores will pay you about ten to thirty percent of what the book is worth—and then turn around and charge next year's poor student eighty percent of the new price. Don't feed this system! Instead, sell by using one of the approaches listed above: use a student-run service, throw up a poster somewhere, or sell them online.

10. Instead of Buying Your Books, Rent Them

Since we finished our undergraduate degrees, the new development in saving students from the campus bookstore has been textbook rentals. Several campuses have private businesses set up to facilitate this option, and there are many larger players online. There are also a few places that have begun to offer e-books that are available for rent during the year. According to what we were able to find online, textbook rentals will usually set you back just twenty-five to forty percent of what the book would cost you if you bought it new. Obviously this opens up many new options for students in the years come. We haven't yet met anyone who has personal experience with this option, but we believe it is a practice that will grow rapidly over the next few years. Renting textbooks appears to be a way to lower costs for the average student while still providing value to textbook manufacturers.

Textbooks are unsexy (even for self-professed book nerds) yet a necessary expense, but they don't have to cripple your budget. This is an area where students' classic procrastination and laziness often get the better of their bank accounts. Students often purchase textbooks at the beginning of terms, when they have the most money in their pockets, not realizing of course that, much of the time, that seasonal surplus of money should be budgeted over the whole school year. It's simply easier to print your book list, march down to the bookstore, and cross them off, than it is to spend an hour or so looking online or making some simple posters. When you consider that the extra hour of effort will almost assuredly keep *hundreds of dollars* from flying into the black hole of textbook spending, it seems like a pretty good deal!

Chapter 13 Summary

- Textbooks are a mandatory expense that can be greatly reduced with a few simple tricks.
- It takes very little effort each semester to save hundreds of dollars in textbooks.
- As to the title of this book: we'd much rather spend money on beer than textbooks.

CHAPTER FOURTEEN
BUT I THOUGHT IT WOULDN'T HAPPEN TO ME (INSURANCE FOR STUDENTS)

DO *not* skip this chapter! Seriously, though, insurance is one thing in life that isn't sexy, isn't going to be something you brag about at happy hour, and won't matter much—until it does. Insurance is integral to your financial life as a young adult.

In our experience, most of us don't even really understand what insurance is about. Many young Canadians simply walk in to an insurance broker's, or talk to a family friend who "knows about that stuff", and then sign on the dotted line.

Actually, the basics of insurance are pretty straightforward.

Insurance is about the risk that expensive bad stuff will happen. Most people want to avoid the possibility of having to pay out of their own pockets to deal with very expensive problems. Those people avoid that possibility by buying insurance **policies**, which are contracts provided by **insurance companies**. (The companies are also called **insurers**.) Sometimes people buy policies through middlemen called **agents** and **brokers**. Someone who buys a policy is a **policyholder**. The price that a policyholder pays for a policy is the **premium**; usually it's broken up into instalments paid annually, semi-annually, quarterly, or monthly. An insurance policy doesn't keep bad stuff from happening, but it does protect against the financial expense of dealing with bad stuff once it happens. These expensive events are called **losses**, and a policy spells out what kinds of losses are **covered** (protected against). If you have insurance and you suffer a loss, you file a **claim** with your insurance agent or company. The company has employees called **claims adjusters**, who confirm that the loss occurred and then write you a cheque to help you deal with the financial hurt. The amount of money you could receive for a certain type of loss is called the **coverage**; it's specified in the policy. When money is paid to you for a loss, it's called the **benefit**.

The basic principle behind insurance has two parts: (1) that it's hard to predict losses with *certainty*—exactly what bad stuff will happen, and exactly where, when, and to whom—and (2) that it's relatively easy to predict the chance that a loss will occur in a given *generalized* situation. Individuals and families can never be sure when they might suffer a loss, and the loss might be so expensive that it would ruin them financially. So they trade the *uncertain chance* of a *ruinous* blow to their finances for a *guaranteed* periodic expense that's much *smaller*—the premium that they pay to have insurance. Because very large numbers of people are all paying relatively small amounts of money to the insurance company at regular intervals—and because the insurance company puts some of that money into investments, where it grows—there is a big pool of funds from which to write benefit cheques to policyholders when they suffer losses.

Insurance companies have access to huge piles of data that their mathematicians, called **actuaries**, use to predict the chance of a loss in a given situation. For example, if you are of a certain age and sex, you own a certain type of car, and you've had no tickets for breaking traffic laws in the last several years, actuaries can predict how likely you are to cause a car accident or have your car stolen. If there's a low risk that a given loss will occur, you'll pay a low premium to get insurance against that risk. On the other hand, if there's a relatively high chance of a loss, your insurance will cost you more. Your premium also depends on the possible costs of the losses you might suffer: if your car would be especially expensive to repair or replace if damaged or stolen, for example, insuring it will cost you more than you would pay to insure a cheaper car.

Even if you never suffer a loss, the money you pay for insurance is not wasted—because it also buys you peace of mind. For example, you can get stuck with the parking-space right under the huge tree on a stormy night without worrying about having to pay out of your own pocket to replace your car if the wind sends the tree crashing down.

Still, it's good to do what you can to reduce risks. A low-risk lifestyle means that you have a lower chance of having to deal with a problem in the first place—and, coupled with insurance, that low-risk lifestyle means that you won't have to pay much to get a big financial benefit if something bad happens anyway.

The rest of this chapter deals with just four types of insurance that are super-smart for students to have: car insurance (including a quick discussion of the **deductible**, which is one other concept that can be found in several types of insurance); tenant's insurance; travel insurance; and medical and dental insurance. As you progress through life, you'll face new possible losses and find an increasing need for insurance against them; at the end of the chapter is a brief table naming some other common types of insurance and the losses they protect against.

CAR INSURANCE

Car insurance is there to cover your butt if you drive a car, ride in one, own one, or are hit by one. Sometimes, when something bad happens to you or your vehicle or your other property, someone else's insurance policy is used to pay for the damage. (Who is this "someone else"? It's the person who, in the eyes of the law, is responsible for the loss that occurred. This is the person who's **at fault**.) At other times, if *you* are at fault, *your* policy pays for the loss—whether it was your own property that was damaged, someone else's property, or both.

Cars are expensive; and they're heavy, powerful, and fast. The damage that can be done to a car, and the damage a car can do to something else (or someone), can be expensive. That's why you need car insurance; in fact, the need for car insurance to deal with these expensive problems is so great that the government requires every car and every driver to be insured. That's true for rentals too.

If a specific other party can be determined to be at fault in a car accident that hurt you or your car, that person's insurance will pay for whatever damage or injury you suffer.

Your own car insurance deals with three kinds of losses: those for which you are at fault, those for which an unknown other person is at fault, and those for which nobody is at fault. If your car is parked sensibly and a naturally falling tree crushes it, the damage is nobody's fault—but you still need money to deal with it. If your car is stolen, the thief is at fault—but you still need money to rent a car while the police do their work and maybe to buy a new one. If you crash your car into something or someone and you're at fault, your insurance will pay the injured party for the loss—whether it's damage to your car, damage to someone else's property, an injury to a person, or some combination of those. In all these cases, your insurance is your saviour.

If you're a young driver, you're going to pay a big premium for car insurance; that's just how it is, because more than a century of automobile use has shown that a disproportionate amount of damage is caused by young drivers. The good news is that, if you keep a clean driving record, you can look forward to a premium that shrinks as you get older. You can also lower your premium by driving less distance per year and by owning a car that's cheaper to repair and replace and has lots of good safety features.

You really have to consider the insurance premium as part of the cost of owning and using a car; premiums for young people, especially, are so high that they can't be ignored. To be smart, get a definite figure for the insurance before you even choose to buy a particular vehicle. If you're thinking of buying one, contact some insurers and get them each to give you a **quote** for your exact situation, including the year, make, and model you're considering. A quote, which usually is good for a set number of days from when it's first given to you, is the company's guarantee of the premium you will pay for the policy if all the information you gave for the quote turns out to be true when you buy the policy.

To avoid the risk of a super-high premium for a policy owned by a young driver, many students make do with the "family car", which is owned and insured by their parents. This also helps on student-loan applications, because the application forms ask you to list your car as an asset if you own one. However, some car-insurance companies are growing increasingly strict about guidelines for student drivers, and they can void an insurance claim if they determine that the policyholder (Mom and Dad) did not have "care, custody, and control of the vehicle the majority of the time". While you should be fine if you live at home, it might be a little more difficult if you're living away from home with a vehicle insured by your parents. We recommend discussing the agreement with your parents and their insurance broker.

Something else to investigate is whether your car insurance should fall under the umbrella of "commuter" or "all-purpose". Because car insurance differs so much from province to province, it is difficult to get into specifics. British Columbia, Manitoba, and Saskatchewan all have car-insurance industries that are run primarily through government-owned entities, whereas the rest of the provinces are split among a variety of private insurance companies.

When you are buying insurance, don't be afraid to ask the broker or company why your premium is what it is. You should be able to get them to explain it clearly to you.

There is another factor that will determine how big or small your premium is. We mentioned it briefly in this chapter's intro. It's the **deductible**. When you file an insurance claim, you also have to pay a certain amount of money from your own pocket to deal with the damage; this money is the deductible. It's usually a fairly small amount, compared to the overall loss. Here's how it works: let's say your car policy includes a $500 deductible, and you get yourself into an accident that damages your car to the tune of $2,000; you'll be responsible for the first $500 of the repair cost, and your insurance company will write you a cheque for the remaining $1,500. Deductibles exist to discourage policyholders from making lots of little claims that would strain the system and make insurance less appealing overall. If, for example, you have a $500 deductible and you have car damage that costs $300 to fix, there's no reason to go through the claims process with your insurance company, because you're responsible for the first $500 of damage anyway. This can be maddening when you have a small dint in your bumper, but it is beneficial in the long run.

How does your deductible affect your premium? If you choose to have a high deductible, your premium will be lower. On the other hand, if you choose to have a low deductible, your premium will be higher. It's a trade-off, a combination of a guessing-game about the future and thoughtful planning. Here are the pros and cons of the two options:

- **A high deductible** means a lower premium, which is nice to have during all that safe driving you've been doing without causing an accident. The premium is low because the insurer has to pay less of your repair cost: if you do have to repair damage to your car, you pay a big chunk out of your own pocket before the insurance money covers the rest. If you choose a high deductible, you'll be smart to make sure you have the full amount of the deductible ready in savings at all times, in case of a loss. If you save on your premium by choosing a $1,000 deductible, but you blow the savings on toys, what will you do when you need $1,200 in repairs to get moving after an accident and the insurance covers only the last $200? Those with enough self-control to set aside the deductible and not touch it should do that, let it earn some interest in the bank, and enjoy a lower premium every month.

- **A low deductible** keeps your out-of-pocket expenses low when you file a claim. With a $200 deductible and a $1,200 wreck, the insurance covers $1,000 of the cost. But a lower deductible means you'll be paying extra regularly in your premium, even if you don't have an accident, just so you can avoid a high deductible if an accident finally occurs. If you'd have trouble resisting the temptation to spend a large amount set aside in savings for a high deductible, choose a lower one until you've matured a bit. Sometimes paying a higher premium in steady monthly payments is easier than resisting the urge to spend a lot of money sitting in the bank. If you need repairs, you'll be glad the insurance will cover everything but the small deductible.

Contents Insurance and Tenant's Insurance

Think of all the stuff inside your house or apartment—the **contents**. Furniture, electronics, appliances, books, clothes, movies, music, tools, instruments, and a zillion other things. These things aren't invincible: they can be damaged, destroyed, lost, and stolen. If you own the house or apartment containing all those things, **homeowner's insurance** usually covers losses involving your stuff, though in some cases you might get separate **contents insurance**.

If you pay rent to a landlord for the house or apartment you live in, or if you live in residence on campus, then the landlord or residence has its own insurance to protect the building and the appliances that aren't owned by the tenants—but that does *not* protect your personal possessions inside. So you should get contents insurance, which in this case is also called **tenant's insurance**.

While in post-secondary education, young students are still

considered their parents' dependants, as far as some tenant's insurance is concerned. This means your contents are usually covered, up to about $10,000, under your parents' policy (check it for the exact amount). Like car policies, tenant's policies have a deductible you must pay before the insurance kicks in for a claim. Contents insurance for students can be used for a number of things, but the main concern is often their computers. Some other items that might be listed are jewellery, furniture, and a set of golf clubs. Many insurance companies give the option of **scheduling** certain items (making a specific, official list of them) to reduce the deductible. Make sure to check with your broker to see whether your parents' policy covers you at school. Some insurance policies even have different coverage rules for students living on campus and those living off campus. If the policy doesn't cover your situation, or if you just graduated and are renting somewhere, *don't try to cut costs by skipping tenant's insurance!* For $10 to $15 a month (about 33 to 50 cents a day), you can save yourself a huge headache in the case of a fire, a robbery, or an "act of God". No matter what people tell you, the landlord's insurance covers only the landlord's property, not yours!

A common tip for anyone with contents insurance or tenant's insurance: keep an itemized list of your valuables in a safe place so that it's easier to make an insurance claim in case of a loss. Serial numbers and descriptions make your life a lot easier if misfortune strikes. These days, with computers, email, online storage, and digital cameras, it's free and easy to make and keep pretty thorough documentation of your valuables. Take photos with your digital camera, email them to yourself, and keep the email in your email account online. Do the same with written descriptions, and with scans of the receipts for major purchases.

Finally, do everything you can to get a policy with coverage for your possessions' **replacement cost**, which is how much money it takes to buy a replacement in the event of a loss. This is different from an object's **market value**, the amount you could get if you tried to sell the object used, which is almost always a lot less than its replacement cost. The market value of your five-year-old sofa is nowhere near what you'd have to pay for a new replacement in case of a loss. Yes, even market-value coverage is better than no coverage at all, but replacement-cost coverage is a *much* better value.

TRAVEL INSURANCE

If you're a student planning to take trips outside of Canada, contact your insurance provider to make sure you have travel insurance. This type of insurance covers you for many medical bills you may have incurred on your trip to Vegas. (Bills for such scenarios as trying to remove your own teeth to prove you can, and laser removal of face tattoos depicting your favourite Heavyweight Champ, are not covered under most policies.) For young adults, this is a small cost—usually around $15 to $20 for a three- or four-day trip to most places. Chances are that the travel office on your local campus will be able to help you. Keep in mind that some credit cards automatically provide travel insurance if you pay for the trip with the card; however, most student cards do not have this premium feature.

MEDICAL AND DENTAL INSURANCE

Many student unions across Canada now automatically charge all students, in their tuition, for insurance plans providing dental and medical coverage. The idea behind this is to get the lowest fees possible for the overall group. However, many young people are covered by their parents' insurance. It's probably worth your time to ask your folks about this. If one of your parents works for the government or a fairly large company, there's a strong possibility that your student union is taking an extra couple hundred bucks from you every year to give you a duplicate insurance product that you don't need! In Kyle's case, his mom was a nurse, so he always opted out of the automatic student coverage: he was covered under her substantial family plan at Blue Cross. If your parents' coverage doesn't include you, though, be thankful for the automatic medical and dental insurance from your school, because it is usually a pretty good deal and could save you from shelling out big bucks for an ambulance ride or a dental emergency.

All That Other Stuff

After graduation, you'll have way more to worry about—and then you can start thinking about stuff like life insurance, disability insurance, and homeowner's insurance . . . but you can cross that bridge when you come to it.

Insurance	Risk
Disability	An injury or illness interferes with your ability to work for a living.
Employment	You lose your job through no fault of your own.
Flood	Similar to homeowner's insurance, but for floods, which most homeowner's insurance doesn't cover.
Health (medical, dental)	You need medical care to prevent or treat an illness or injury.
Homeowner's (home, house, housing)	A fire or other peril damages or destroys the home you own. (Usually includes contents insurance and liability insurance.)
Liability	You lose a costly lawsuit. This general category overlaps others, such as car and homeowner's.
Life	You die, and your family has funeral expenses to pay and has lost the income you were providing.
Old-age pension	You grow too old to work.
Property	Property that you own is damaged, destroyed, lost, or stolen. This general category overlaps others, such as car, homeowner's, and tenant's.
Tenant's (contents, renter's)	You rent your dwelling from a landlord, and your property inside the dwelling is damaged, destroyed, lost, or stolen.
Travel	Bad stuff happens while you're traveling far from home.

Chapter 14
Summary

- You never get excited about insurance—until you need it.
- You pay for insurance in two ways: deductibles and premiums.
- Check your parents' homeowner's insurance to see whether it covers you. If it doesn't, tenant's insurance should be a priority.
- If you ignored the chapter on owning a car and now own one, become familiar with vehicle insurance. You want to make sure your policy has ample coverage at a competitive price.
- Before you're "wheels up", grab some travel insurance.
- If you are already covered by private medical and dental insurance policies (either through your own policy or that of a parent), make sure your student union isn't taking a few hundred bucks out of your pocket every year for insurance you don't need.

CHAPTER FIFTEEN
THE IMPORTANCE OF CHOOSING AN IN-DEMAND CAREER

LET'S do a quick little case study. For argument's sake, let's say Student A and Student B start at similar spots in life and have similar resources to draw upon.

- Student A reads MORE MONEY FOR BEER AND TEXTBOOKS and faithfully implements all of the tips and advice, getting scholarships, sticking to a budget, landing great summer jobs, and generally doing quite well. Upon graduation, Student A has no debt and maybe even has some meagre savings.

- Student B decides that actually consuming beer while using textbooks for coasters sounds like a much better use of time than reading anything that has to do with stuff like *shiver* budgeting. This student takes out the maximum student loans, manages to use up an $8,000 SLOC, and parties so hard that school takes an extra year. Finally, Student B even has *gasp* credit-card debt when donning the famous cap and gown.

Now what sort of scenario would lead Student A to be quite far *behind* Student B five years after their graduations? If Student A took a wide variety of liberal-arts courses and didn't establish any specific career while in school, and Student B became an engineer or went into a high-demand trade, such as those in the electrical field or carpentry, then this scenario isn't as crazy as it at first sounds. The importance of getting all the facts before making a decision about post-secondary education cannot be overstated. As educational costs continue to rise, making an informed decision about what kind of education the market is calling for has become more important than ever before.

Several Degrees of Difference

We're definitely going to take some heat for being so open about this, but the truth is that not all higher-education options are created equal, as far as earning-potential goes. In fact, they're not even close. In generations past, getting a university degree of any kind was enough to secure advantageous employment for a lifetime. Make no mistake: those days are long gone. Before all you people with liberal-arts degrees (hey, we have them too!) try to email us extremely well worded and grammatically perfect complaint letters documenting how you have "soft skills" and critical-thinking abilities, just allow us to present a few facts.

Compensation packages (pay, wages, salaries) are not determined merely by who is smartest or who has the most education. The free market is based on supply and demand. The more people with certain types of arts degrees there are on the market, the less demand there is to hire any specific one of them. We're not here to make philosophical judgements on what educational path is intrinsically better or morally superior: we're simply stating the economic facts of today's market. The Canadian Department of Finance has released statistics showing that, in fields such as business, mathematics, and engineering, graduates earn twelve to seventeen percent of the upfront cost of their education every year, meaning it takes only about six to eight years to earn back all the money you spent on school. The social sciences and humanities came in at four to six percent: it takes about twenty years to earn back the money you spent on school. This is just the start of a pool of data that doesn't look good for us liberal-arts students. (Luckily we don't know how to read pools of data, so we can continue to make well reasoned and well communicated arguments about how valuable we are.)

Statistics Canada also recently presented information showing that humanities students were the least likely to find work in fields directly related to their education. In other words, while many arts students *are* finding employment after graduation, they often are *underemployed* or are forced by economic circumstances to get jobs in fields they hadn't planned to work in. According to a recent report in *The Globe and Mail*, Quebec research company CIRANO has found that "degree and certificate holders in specialized fields are significantly more likely to have employment directly related to their education, while 31 per cent of humanities graduates are currently employed in fields not at all related to their education." That number is pretty tough to argue with.

A study by the Certified General Accountants Association of Canada, *Youth Unemployment in Canada: Challenging Conventional Thinking?*, came to the same conclusion—that many people with bachelor's degrees are underemployed, if they are working at all. The report states that 24.6 percent of youth with university degrees who were employed full-time throughout 2005 were doing jobs that didn't require university education and that the condition was "particularly prevalent" among those with bachelor's degrees. What's even scarier is that the figure doesn't include those youth who were unemployed, absent from the job market for various reasons, and employed only part-time. That rate, nearly one in four, probably would be higher if it didn't include people with graduate degrees in addition to their bachelor's degrees, whose higher employment rates lower the average. Finally, the global economic recession of 2008–2009 has probably caused these trends to accelerate. Given those realities, we find it is reasonable to assume the youth unemployment rate is substantially higher today—and looks especially ugly for those holding bachelor-of-*arts* degrees.

Remember Rob Carrick, from CHAPTER 1? He's the personal-finance columnist from *The Globe and Mail*; he's also the author of *How Not to Move Back In with Your Parents: The Young Person's Guide to Financial Empowerment*. Mr. Carrick is adamant that more students need to understand the economic reality of pursuing certain types of post-secondary education before they commit to that education. He has written often about a public education system that fails to teach the truths of the modern job market to the next generation. He also is critical of post-secondary institutions that are not preparing students for that market, and he specifically notes that colleges generally are doing a better job of this than their university counterparts.

The *Globe and Mail* writer is not the only canary in the coal mine, however. Lauren Friese is the founder of *TalentEgg.ca*, a popular website built to help Canadian students find work both during post-secondary study and upon graduation. Ms. Friese recently published in *The Globe and Mail* an article aptly titled "Why Are We Training Our Arts Grads to Be Baristas?" In it, she quotes Adelle Farrelly, who studied at the University of Toronto: "'No one told me that an English degree was not an acceptable prerequisite for even the most basic grunt positions.'" Ms. Farrelly also said, "'When I finished my MA I found myself working at a coffee chain surrounded by fellow graduates and recent graduates, all of us looking for that "real job" and confused about our fate. Remember: Those you see behind the coffee counter are likely a plucky crew of medievalists, statisticians, architects and management graduates.'" Ms. Farrelly is far from the only recently graduated student to express such sentiment. Canada's major newspapers (in fact many newspapers across the Western World) are awash in stories of students whose frustration at the magnitude of their student-loan debt is exceeded only by their despair at their odds of becoming gainfully employed.

THE PROBLEM WITH A LIBERAL-ARTS DEGREE

The overarching problem with a generalized liberal-arts degree today is that many students are becoming educated in topics that interest them, or taking courses that they complete relatively easily, but doing it *without having any semblance of a plan to translate that knowledge and that credential into any sort of career*. There is nothing wrong with taking a liberal-arts course load simply for the love of learning the subject matter; but students need to realize that they are paying money to take courses for that reason, as opposed to getting an education that will give them the skills the job market now demands. In saying that, we should be clear that not all liberal-arts degrees are created equal, and in researching this book we found that many different definitions of the liberal arts exist. Degrees with majors such as film, philosophy, theatre, psychology, sociology, and even some of those social sciences such as economics and political science (two of Kyle's personal favorites) often do not lead directly to jobs. Many would say they don't even point you to where the jobs might be!

To the credit of most universities, they are largely consistent (when directly asked) about the fact that the liberal-arts education they provide is *not* inherently tied to the economy's supply-and-demand compensation structure (i.e., finding a high-paying job). Instead, most Canadian universities state some variation of the fact that their goal is to broaden students' intellectual horizons and allow them to explore "soft skills", such as problem-solving and communication strategies. Such phrases as "critical thinking" and "well rounded" also are often peppered into the conversation.

The problem of today's Canadian job market, in which workers' skill sets do not match those required for the most numerous positions, is the result of too many young adults' believing that any liberal-arts degree will directly qualify them for "good jobs". While liberal-arts faculties officially state that their role in society is not to train students for specific jobs, they also don't do much to dispel the widespread myth (which became popular in quite a different era) that their product and the credential they can bestow upon you will greatly help in your finding a "good job" when you've graduated.

In the past, parents encouraged their children to attend university no matter what. Their attitude was justified by the relatively cheap tuition and the fact that people with almost any liberal-arts degree had a ticket they could cash in for the rest of their lives. These days, those tickets pay neither nearly as well nor nearly as consistently as they once did. The aforementioned study by the Certified General Accountants Association of Canada has a whole section headlined "The Labour Market Advantage of Higher Education Is Diminishing"—and it doesn't list any reason why this might change. High-schoolers are told that university is the one place to pursue higher education and that it will help fulfill their hopes and dreams if they work hard enough. This is simply no longer true. When you combine this misplaced pressure from parents, and from the public education system, with the relative quiet of universities (who are searching to maximize enrollment, after all), you get students believing in a reality that simply no longer exists.

THOSE WHO CAN'T DO . . .

One area where the over-saturation of liberal-arts degrees can be seen and easily quantified is the field of education—at all levels. As a high-school teacher, Kyle can speak with some authority on the fact that the job market in education is *tough* right now. To give you some idea: in 2010, the Ontario College of Teachers (OCT) reported that two thirds of its graduates were unemployed or underemployed in their first year after graduation, and that number had been rising at least four years. Many of OCT's graduates entered the school only when they realized that the liberal-arts degrees they had spent several years earning were not enough to get them the well paying jobs they wanted. Teaching is one of the few areas where they can directly apply their prior education. In addition to that dynamic, there's also the fact that many students who don't quite have the grades to get into professional faculties, such as law, see teaching as their logical "fallback" option. Instead of consciously looking at the employment statistics being generated and limiting their class sizes accordingly, faculties of education across Canada are placing on students the onus to incorporate the situation's supply-and-demand reality into their plans. The result is a large (and growing) body of desperate young teachers who specialize in liberal-arts areas that are not in demand and who don't have job prospects in proportion to either the size of their student loans or the huge time commitment they made to get their liberal-arts degrees.

The statistics for the student who chooses to sacrifice several years of earning-potential in order to get a Ph.D. are not much better. Having *several dozen* applicants for every *one* liberal-arts-based university teaching gig that pops open is the new norm. In many instances, working hard and "blindly" attaining higher academic credentials is just not enough to get ahead anymore. You also must consider the basic math behind a supply-and-demand market.

SOFT SKILLS AND A SOFT JOB MARKET

To further complicate the issue, the "soft skills" on which many liberal-arts faculties have commonly hung their hat are no longer gained exclusively in the university classroom, no matter what your professor or university administrator says. Technology is offering stiff competition to classrooms that are routinely packed past their filling-points at major universities. Online universities are steadily increasing in number and, beyond that, the Internet in general is limiting any informational advantage that the ivory towers once enjoyed semi-exclusively (especially in the liberal arts). Such websites as *KhanAcademy.org* and those run by major academic icons, including Harvard University and the Massachusetts Institute of Technology, are free resources that all kinds of people can use to challenge themselves and become smarter. Given that credentials in many of the humanities and social sciences are steadily being devalued in terms of job prospects, and given that the cost of these educational options is rising, the cost–benefit ratio of a university liberal-arts degree is looking worse and worse.

We're not really "math people"; we don't consider an education in math and science to be intrinsically superior to a liberal-arts education; and we definitely don't have a private agenda. Kyle even teaches humanities to students every day, and is proud of his Bachelor of Arts degree. A university degree in a liberal-arts field is still a great achievement in an educational sense; and a person is still better off having a liberal-arts degree that not having one, all things being equal. But not all other things *are* equal, for a liberal arts-degree requires considerable amounts of time and money to get; and we would be doing a disservice to the readers of our book if we did not shine a light on the fact that not all post-secondary educations are created equal, as far as the job market is concerned.

If you want to pursue knowledge for the sake of becoming smarter, if you want to develop the "soft skills" mentioned above, and if you want to have a great time and focus on self-development, then you should pursue a liberal-arts education with all the passion you can muster. If you want a path to a well paying career that is in demand at the moment, however, there are arguably much more sensible paths to take than the winding obstacle course that your liberal-arts degree provides.

With the financial costs of post-secondary education rising higher and higher, students face increasing pressure to make proper long-term decisions at an age when long-term planning consists of taking frozen food out in the morning so it can thaw in time for dinner. We honestly believe that, with a solid book list, a book club, a couple of decent literary-discussion forums, and supplemental lectures found on the Internet (often from ultra-high-quality speakers), many of the goals of a liberal-arts *education* can be achieved for a tiny fraction of the cost that universities charge you for a liberal-arts *degree*. The unfortunate economic truth that confronts us is that becoming a major in the field of post-modern dance-inspired jazz therapy while minoring in neo-political gender-neutralizing navel-gazing simply is not a good career choice. If you have the financial resources to take these courses as a luxury and for all the legitimate reasons listed above—then go for it. If you ever want to take part in our money-dominated society, however, you probably should look at an education that actually will lead to a job you can live on.

WHY NOT SKILLED LABOUR FOR LITTLE JOHNNY AND JANE?

After reading a history major's sermon on why not to pay for a history degree, most of you are probably shaking your heads. Here is some more food for thought: an Ipsos Reid survey in 2004 reported that sixty-seven percent of youth aged thirteen to twenty-four, and fifty-five percent of adults, stated that university was their first choice for education; the more alarming statistic is that only twenty-six percent of respondents said that they would consider a career in the skilled trades. Yet, in October 2010, Statistics Canada reported that employees in the trades earned an average hourly wage of $22.36—which is six percent higher than the average Canadian's hourly wage. Today's attitude also ignores the fact that the Canadian Federation of Independent Business has reported shortage of skilled labour as a big concern facing independent businesses. Finally, in a Manpower global survey in 2012, skilled labour topped the list of the world's high-demand jobs, the fourth time in five consecutive years. If not only the demand but also *the compensation* are there, why don't young Canadians know about it?

Chances are that you were told by most of the educational authorities in your life that going to university was the first step that all financially successful and respectable people took these days. In the aforementioned Ipsos Reid survey, seventy-two percent of youth polled said that their school guidance counsellors did not encourage careers in the trades. We can say with absolute certainty that trades and skilled-labour careers do not get a fair shake in our education system. Part of the bias comes simply from the traditional stereotype that skilled labour is "dirty", relatively low-paying, and definitely less prestigious than white-collar work. Most of the bias, however, is sort of structurally built in to the very DNA of our education system: except perhaps the "shops" or industrial-arts specialists in some cases, every teacher and administrator in our schools went through the university system. More and more of them swam the liberal-arts streams to get there (go ahead and walk in to an elementary school and see how many teachers there have any math background at all). When you look at it logically, how could there *not* be an overall deficit of enthusiasm and knowledge surrounding skilled labour in our academic system?

These stereotypes and biases are no longer relevant in today's job market. While the *average* trades worker might earn six percent above the Canadian average, we think there is a very strong argument to be made that certain areas of skilled labour are earning workers much more than that (especially for workers willing to relocate). To give even a subtle impression that a trades-based post-secondary education is "dirty" or somehow less dignified than certain paths of university education is ridiculous. Many types of knowledge are required to make society function, and right now the basic supply-and-demand math is telling us that there is a surplus of one area of skills and a deficit of another.

A recent article by Kathryn Blaze Carlson in the *National Post* quoted a professor at San Diego State University, in California: "'A lot of (young graduates) feel like they were sold a bill of goods—that they were told if they go to university and get a degree, that they'll get a job. Young people feel like nobody ever told them how hard it was going to be, and I think they have a point.'" If you go through school and amass loads of debt without having a plan for how to get a job you can live on from that credential you're working so hard for, life will be very frustrating indeed.

Here's a final sales point on skilled-labour careers. (And, yes, the irony of liberal-arts graduates' putting their education to use in writing about how great skilled-labour jobs are is not lost on us.) The big worry in the North American job market today is that your job could be outsourced—that you will be fired because someone in another country has been hired to take over your job and do the work there. While many sectors of our economy are taking a beating at the hands of cheap labour around the world, it is extremely difficult to outsource skilled-labour jobs (with the exception of those in manufacturing). The skilled-labour shortage is fairly consistent across most of the world, so there isn't nearly as much competition in this field as there is in others.

Finally—and this is true especially if you're willing to work in rural Canada—this overall trend seems unlikely to stop anytime soon. While there is a substantial number of young teachers chomping at the heels of the outgoing baby-boomers, that is not the case in the trades. As the generational behemoth in front of us begins to enter its golden years, whoever is there to pick up their wrench, hammer, and blueprints is going to be well situated. If those of you making the wise choice to get into the skilled trades can add a bit of a business background to your résumés as you go, you'll be laughing at us white-collar folk all the way to the bank.

FACTS AND INCENTIVES

We're not saying that a math- or trades-based education is better overall than one in the liberal arts. That is an impossible question to answer, and the "truth" will be different for everyone. We just want students to be fully aware of the reality in today's marketplace and to be able to make their own educated decisions about what post-secondary studies they want to pursue.

The latest statistics tell us that going to school is a great thing in any economy and that people with liberal-arts degrees are still generally better off than people with no post-secondary degree at all. If the only way you'll be happy is to work in a liberal-arts field, then the economics are irrelevant: you should do what leaves you satisfied at the end of the day.

At the same time, we need to do a better job of preparing and informing our young people for the modern economy. Ms. Friese recently wrote, in the *National Post*, "Students need to step up and realize that a career is not just going to happen to them. They need to plan." Pushing more and more people towards the "university at all costs" mindset is not the answer. If you choose an educational path that is in low demand as far as the job market is concerned, it is not a career death sentence: it simply means that you have to work extra hard to make yourself a standout candidate within your field, and you must have a Plan B (and C, D, etc.) to market yourself, and you have to be flexible.

On the bright side for many of you gentlemen out there: as women make up a larger and larger percentage of the university student body, a liberal-arts degree has literally never looked more attractive! By the same token, we'd be willing to bet the social dynamics would be pretty favourable to young ladies with an interest in the trades as well. ☺

Chapter 15
Summary

- Not all post-secondary education is created equal in the eyes of the free market.
- Students need more accurate information about future job prospects and the state of the labour force in order to make optimal decisions. Schools and parents both need to make this a priority.
- Many scholars and post-secondary institutions believe that the goal of a liberal-arts education is simply to give people a well rounded education after high school. Many students believe that the goal of a liberal-arts education should be to provide them with the skills and credentials to succeed in the job market. There is a fundamental contradiction there.
- Basic humanities degrees are not as valuable on average as they used to be.
- Math and science aren't getting any easier, and consequently they don't seem to be going out of demand either.
- Trades-based credentials are substantially more valuable on average than they used to be.

INTO THE "REAL WORLD"

DON'T you love how teachers and other adults are always lecturing you about how afraid you should be of the "real world"? The truth is that this scary image of insurmountable obstacles and danger lying in wait around every corner is a little overblown—as long as you plan for it. If you refuse to learn and adapt as you go through post-secondary education and enter the working world, then you might be setting yourself up for some pretty hard knocks. On the other hand, if you take a little time to plan beyond the party next weekend, the "real world" can be a pretty attractive place, which you'll probably find fairly rewarding.

This book was never meant to be the be-all and end-all of your personal-finance education. Basically, we're just trying to help the young adults we work with every day, and those like them, to understand a few key things that will allow them to enter the workforce with the wind at their backs and without a massive ball-and-chain of debt at their ankles. If people believe that what we're writing about is worth reading, there definitely could be another book in the works. After all, as long as our education system determines that personal finance is a fringe topic at best, there will be a large demand for other sources of "real world" information.

In the mean time, if you're looking to take the next step in your financial journey, we recommend these resources:

- *The Wealthy Barber: Everyone's Commonsense Guide to Becoming Financially Independent*, by David Chilton
- *The Wealthy Barber Returns: Dramatically Older and Marginally Wiser, David Chilton Offers His Unique Perspectives on the World of Money*, by D-Chill
- *The Millionaire Teacher: The Nine Rules of Wealth You Should Have Learned in School*, by Andrew Hallam
- A few good books and fascinating articles in the BIBLIOGRAPHY, starting on page 209
- Our Canadian blogging friends, whom you can find through Justin's sites—*MyUniversityMoney.com* and *YoungandThrifty.ca*

We know that sounded like the part of a textbook labelled "For Further Study", which everyone flips right by; but, if you want to really give yourself a financial head start in life, those are excellent places to begin.

If you're a young adult who just graduated or is beginning to see that light at the end of the tunnel, we definitely recommend bringing yourself up to speed on such topics as financial planning, investing, major purchases, career-building, handling debt, and even retirement. Yes, we know that you just graduated and that retirement is a laughable concept at the moment; but the younger you start thinking about this stuff, the more time and arithmetic you'll have on your side. Of course we should give Justin's websites one last plug here, because we touch on these topics (in the least boring way possible) every week: if you take a quick look through the archives at *YoungandThrifty.ca/archive/* and *MyUniversityMoney.com/post-list/* you'll find a bevy of great articles that you can search through quickly in order to find what you're looking for.

A last note of advice to people entering the infamous "real

world": don't succumb to the barrage of consumerism that will be aimed at you in the next few years. Companies love to target graduates who are getting their first taste of a steady paycheque and believe they should treat themselves after all their frugal years of study. Don't fall into the debt trap the day you leave post-secondary education. Yes, you are "worth it"—but that doesn't mean you have to buy the latest everything simply because some *Mad Men* types from Manhattan think up a cool way to sell it to you.

THANKS FOR STOPPING BY

Roughly two hundred pages later, we hope you got something out of this. (If nothing else, the beer quotes alone were worth the price of admission, right?) Let us know what you think of More Money for Beer and Textbooks: at *MyUniversityMoney.com/contact-us/* you can drop us a line.

If you have any questions or think we might be able to help you in any way, let us know. We wouldn't be working in the careers we're in, or spending our leisure hours writing a book to help young people, if we didn't sincerely care about them. Chances are that if you have a question there are probably dozens, if not thousands, of other students across Canada who have been wrestling with the same quandary. That goes double if you think it's a stupid question.

Financial concerns have always had a huge effect on students' lives, and these issues are becoming more and more important every day. Don't believe you have to attack this mountain on your own, and don't let financial stuff force you into places you don't want to be in and probably don't have to be in. Cheers for not being like most people and for not sticking your head in the sand in the hope that it will somehow all work out by magic. Give yourself a pat on the back for flipping through a personal-finance book (even if our beer reference on the cover was a dirty trick!).

Finally, in the words of a true Canadian classic, "*More beers, more cheers, that's it, that's all.*"

APPENDIX A
TOP TEN RÉSUMÉ TIPS

THE first thing that you have to realize is that there is no one-size-fits-all tip for résumé writing. Your résumé should adapt to the job you're applying for. For example, most online résumé-building sites suggest putting your education at the top of your résumé, but for Kyle, a teacher, that was basically a waste of time: it was safe to assume that everyone applying for the job was a registered teacher and consequently had a Bachelor of Education degree so, unless he had a master's degree, there was no use listing formal education anywhere near the top. The guidelines below are general concepts that you should consider and adapt to your specific job application.

1. The vast majority of your applications will be looked at for less than thirty seconds.

When administrators are screening the initial pile of applicants for a job, they definitely will not have the patience to read thoroughly a hundred full-length résumés. Instead, they will skim the first half to three quarters of a page in order to pick just a few applicants to put on a short list for further consideration. Your initial résumé goal is to get onto that short list and then into the interview. Keep that "big picture" in focus as you put your résumé together. Ask yourself what makes you unique and what you want to highlight about yourself that will make you stand out from the other applicants. That's the stuff that should go right under your name and contact information.

2. Don't make your résumé any longer than one double-sided page.

This goes along with the time crunch mentioned in Tip 1. We've heard many stories of CEO types who simply throw out stapled résumés as a way to save time. Unless you're applying for an upper-management position, chances are that a multi-page résumé will simply convey that you are not concise, not efficient in promoting yourself—which leads to the idea that you're inefficient in other areas too. View some online samples for tricks to get it all in. Don't worry about making it too short: prospective employers should have all your contact info (at the top of your résumé and on your cover letter) in case they want to know more about you. To us, presenting a one-page résumé to someone also just seems more professional and 'crisper', but that's just our opinion.

3. Squishing information in is not worth it.

When someone is only going to skim your résumé, it's best not to pack the first part with line after line of text. Ask yourself whether it's visually appealing by looking at it. If you believe you *must* get a lot of pertinent information across, do it on the back. Usually, this part will be read only if you have been short-listed anyway (when you already have their attention). Make sure you have appealing spacing between sections, and good margins; experiment with varying amounts of white space and see what looks best.

4. Fresh eyes.

Get someone else to read your résumé and give you some feedback; rinse and repeat. The more opinions you get on your résumé, the more patterns you can pick out. Don't try to incorporate everyone's opinions, because you'll drive yourself crazy with all the contradictory advice. Instead, ask about specific things and try to pick out patterns in those responses. In many cases, you won't know in advance which person will be reviewing your application or what his or her biases will be, but you can plan for the law of averages by eliminating aspects of your résumé that many different types of people pick out as negative and by emphasizing the aspects that have gotten positive reactions from many people. Other people can also help you proofread. This is extremely important, because mistakes in English usage are almost universal causes to throw out otherwise brilliant résumés.

5. Look at your résumé upside-down.

Perhaps the coolest and most unusual tip either of us was ever told was to flip the résumé upside-down. Once you've looked at your résumé long enough, you tend to grow attached, or at least accustomed, to whatever format you've invested so much time in; this makes it very hard to look at it objectively. Flipping it upside-down makes it much easier to pick out problems with organization and spacing: you can focus better on general aesthetics when you're not re-reading your individual words for the millionth time. It also will tell you what parts of the résumé your eye is naturally drawn to. Obviously you want to make sure that the eye is drawn to things you want to highlight. When we get a first impression of an object, there is a lot of subconscious activity that goes into forming the initial thoughts. Looking at a résumé upside-down gives you a great test run of how appealing your design is.

6. Draft a unique cover letter for each position.

Most people generate generic cover letters to use repeatedly when they're applying for jobs. That is exactly the opposite of what you should do. Your goal is not to look the same as everyone else; it's not to give the impression that you want the job exactly as much as everyone else does. Your goal is to stand out, to separate yourself from the pack. Some key phrases can be reused in your cover letters, but also try to add something personal in each one, even if it's something like "I am familiar with the business of _____ because of _____, and I look forward to learning more about it." Always list your contact information in the letterhead and at the end of your cover letter. List all the good phone numbers to reach you at and your email address. There is nothing more frustrating for an administrator with 101 things to do than not being able to contact an applicant. If you want the job, commit to being easy to reach.

7. Put a face to the paper, or at least a personal touch.

If the place you're applying to is within an hour or so of your usual haunts, it cannot be overestimated how much a personal appearance can mean to a potential employer. Anytime somebody can "put a face to a name" when reading your résumé, you increase the chances that you will get on the short list. (This doesn't mean sending a picture with your résumé, which is neither common nor advisable.) Showing up in person allows you to make a positive impression on the secretary or receptionist, who may ultimately determine whether your résumé ever gets seen or not. By appearing humble, confident, polite, and ambitious (just showing up in person communicates that), you can greatly increase your chances of a positive impression. If you can't make it in person (many of the jobs we applied for were well over 100 kilometres away), at least call to make sure your email, fax, or letter was received. When phoning, make sure to put your best foot forward and politely seek confirmation that your résumé went through. Being courteous and appreciative to secretaries is a tip for life—period—and it definitely counts when a job is on the line.

8. Work your connections.

In many lines of work, job openings are never posted publicly. Some sources state that more than half of all jobs are landed through personal connections. Your contacts from all walks of life can help you not only in learning about the job opening, but also in getting your résumé into the short-list pile. A simple walk by and mention of you as a worthy candidate, or a casual name-drop in daily conversation, will automatically make the person in charge take a closer look at your qualifications (which ultimately is what you want). Don't forget to thank the people who spread the word about you. We found a Thank You accompanied by a personalized adult beverage was usually well received.

9. Use high-quality paper and make sure to proofread, Proofread, PROOFREAD!

Using high-quality paper and envelopes is an easy way to give your résumé and cover letter a slight edge in natural first impressions. Good résumé paper is a little thicker and more substantial, won't wrinkle, and has a nice slightly off-white colour, as opposed to the bright bleached colour of regular printer paper. It may not make a difference ninety percent of the time, but it is an easy way to appear professional and to help your chances the other ten percent. Also, always make sure you have plenty of résumés on hand. At mere cents a copy, it's a worthy investment just to print a hundred or so. You never want to be caught short: it looks ridiculous. Always take multiple copies to interviews, so that if you're being interviewed by a panel each person can have a copy. Again, looking prepared and professional is key. Always have one of your résumés with you when you're job-hunting, because you never know when the opportunity may strike. A handshake and handing over a résumé can be all it takes. One point bears repeating: using all these tips carries almost no weight if you have proofreading mistakes in your résumé. We refuse to give this point its own place in this list because to us it's common sense. Don't be the person who misses out on jobs because of a misplaced apostrophe!

10. Learn to promote yourself.

Most people use the cliché "You have to learn how to sell yourself." Maybe we have dirty minds, but this phrase inevitably makes us think briefly of "the world's oldest profession", so we prefer to use the term "promote". Regardless of terminology, it is important to realize that there is a fine line between being humble and not fully representing all you have to offer. Research the best language to use in a résumé. Try to avoid sayings that are too common, such as "Works well independently". Instead, try something more specific, such as "My past employers recognized a strong skill set that allowed me to work independently in a variety of settings and situations." Paying a relatively small fee for a résumé professional's help may not be a bad idea if you are not confident in your vocabulary and description skills. If you do not promote yourself to sound as well matched to the position as possible, chances are that somebody else will. Guess who will end up getting the interview.

Writing a résumé can seem like a monumental exercise. Somehow, you have to boil down everything you have ever done (that you're willing to make public, anyway) into one double-sided page. That's an intimidating task for anyone. Our advice is to start well ahead of time. In fact, start right now! When people are rushed, they make stupid mistakes and do not have time to go through the proper drafting and refinement cycles that ultimately yield the best product. When Kyle started writing his résumé, he hadn't looked at it in years, so it wasn't updated at all. No matter where you are in life, try to take a few minutes every now and again to update your résumé so you don't forget to include pertinent new information. To give you an idea of the timeline: Kyle started working on his résumé in December for the job applications he would be looking at in April through August. From December through February, he probably spent fifty or more hours collecting information for his résumé, reorganizing it, and gathering opinions on it. We can't say that we know for sure that all that work made a difference, but we do know that Kyle got several interviews and eventually was offered a full-time position in a hyper-competitive job market. For us, that is at least some proof that the time is worth it and makes a difference.

APPENDIX B
THE DIRTY DOZEN INTERVIEW TIPS

1. Interviewers hire not necessarily the most qualified candidate, but the one who thinks the most like them.

A friend gave us this tip and it definitely changed our perspective on the interview process. Our goal used to be to impress interviewers with our qualifications so much that they would have no choice but to hire us. With so much competition these days, it's important to realize that there will be other well qualified people also applying for your potential job, and chances are that the position will go to the candidate who makes the best *personal* connection to those conducting the interview. Your goal should be to appear to think like the people interviewing you, because that is ultimately the kind of person they want to work with and the one they'll determine to be "the best fit for the job". A great example of this is the interview that landed Kyle his current job. During the interview, one of the interviewers agreed with one of Kyle's answers and summed it up with a quote from a college basketball coach. Kyle mentioned that he knew the source of the quote, and quite suddenly his interviewer engaged him in a brief tangent about college basketball. That tangent almost certainly stuck in his mind, and subconsciously his opinion of Kyle as someone he would like to work with probably rose substantially. Of course, making up nonexistent similarities probably will backfire in the long run: even if your interviewers don't immediately see through your ploy, you nonetheless will have a hard time enjoying a job where your bosses don't think like you or where you're constantly trying to seem to be someone other than your real self. But the fact is most people have far more things in common than differences, and all it takes is keeping an ear out for that common ground to start building a bridge of noticed similarities between you and your interviewers.

2. The casual time at the beginning of an interview is extremely important.

Everyone will tell you that first impressions are important, but the first five minutes of an interview go beyond that. In fact, if you're really good, first impressions can begin before you even meet your interviewers. In most cases there will be someone to greet you, such as a secretary or receptionist. By being polite with these people and striking up casual conversation, not only can you leave a great impression on them, but also you may learn something about the job or company that you might be able to work in to the interview. The more familiar you seem from the very beginning with all the characters involved and what they spend eight hours of their day working on, the better your chances.

Once you're in the interview, there is usually a casual introductory period in which everyone gets situated and acquainted. Try to take stock of the little things during this brief stretch of time. You want to act like a poker shark, picking up on subtle details. For example, maybe you realize that they have been interviewing all day—so you could preface one of your answers with "I realize you all have had a long day, so I will keep this brief." Another example is picking up on a hobby or a hometown that you can work in to an answer later. We often advise people to look for a sports or music analogy if they can tell that's what their interviewer is into.

3. Do some preliminary research.

Researching ahead of an interview used to be time-consuming and tedious. You had to visit a business casually, search old news clippings, or rely on a broad network of personal connections, to get information about the company and persons who were in your interview. These days, you just have to use that handy search engine! A quick search of where you're applying, and who probably will be in the room with you, can't hurt. When Kyle was applying with school divisions, he would look up their motto, what schools were in the division (other than the one he was applying to), check out what they liked to highlight on their website, and maybe even skim the minutes of the last school-board meeting to see what issues were relevant at the time. Then he would run a quick Google search on the superintendent of the division and on the principal of the school he was applying at. Often he found snippets or quotes of their views on education and related topics. You can also find out whether they are part of a golf club or were awarded a medal for music. This can really help in your quest to find common ground. To be blunt, this will tell you want they want to hear.

4. Answer honestly and use specific examples, tied to the present situation—not vague clichés.

One of the easiest ways to separate a serious candidate from a wannabe is to see who uses canned, cliché, vague answers that reveal little actual concrete information about the candidate. Those who cite specific instances and prove they can think critically about a situation they're in stand in stark contrast. We've unfortunately seen many people prepare for an interview by memorizing answers from websites and subsequently say something like "My biggest weakness is that I am a workaholic—I give too much to my job." A cliché answer like that might make the rest of the interview moot. Instead, look up some of the common questions asked in general and in your specific field, and think of relevant experience you can call upon from previous jobs or volunteer positions. This will help you reply with much more confidence and substance behind your answers.

5. The time for your questions at the end of the interview can be what separates you from the pack.

If you're being interviewed in a competitive field (and these days who isn't?), chances are that at least a couple of the other candidates have done their homework and know what they are doing. This means that it's the little things in an interview that can make the difference. Often it becomes the less formal aspects of the interview, such as the standard "Any questions?" at the end, that make the difference. This is your chance to show that you took the initiative and learned something about the business or organization where you're being interviewed. Asking about a mentorship program and other supports that would be available in your first year shows that you are serious about succeeding in the long term at the position and are not merely attracted by a paycheque. A standard question Kyle used in interviewing for teacher positions was "I am fairly familiar with some of the schools in this division (insert anecdote here), but what would you say are the real strengths of (insert school-division name here)? What sets them apart?" Inevitably the answer would be some generic jargon answer that had no real relevance to anyone, but he could see from the looks on their faces that the question had scored points. It showed that Kyle had a real interest in the bigger work picture and was not just desperate to get hired.

6. As Kyle's high-school basketball coach always said, "If it begins at 3 o'clock, you're late as of 2:51."

This is common sense to us. If either of us were an administrator who had worked his way up the food chain, had 101 things to do, and had multiple interviews to get through in a day, we would rarely if ever hire someone who showed up late to the interview. Our athletic coaches never took "No" for an answer, and it was a positive life lesson. What we often do for job interviews is give ourselves one hour's slack time from ideal driving-conditions. This way, if we encounter any bad weather, heavy traffic, or detours, we should still be fine. If you get there early, just use the time to review once more your résumé, portfolio, and any other relevant information, so that you are "in the zone". We recommend walking in fifteen minutes early, so that you're not a nuisance by being too early but you also show the level of respect that the process deserves. It also gives a good amount of time to make small talk with the secretary or receptionist and leave a positive impression, yet not be a hindrance to his or her work.

7. Dress appropriately.

Duh. We hesitated even to include this tip, because, if you have taken the time to read this far, you're probably not the type of person to go to an interview wearing board shorts and a T-shirt. It's not just about the impression you make on others: feeling underdressed can quickly sap *your* self-confidence. Look up what "appropriate interview attire" is for your field and prospective position. As a couple of guys who admittedly have about as much fashion sense as your average "he needs a makeover" reality-show contestant, we get people who are more fashion-conscious to give us feedback. Finally, use some common sense and don't wear overpowering scents, such as strong perfume or cologne, or wear "loud" jewellery that will draw attention away from your brilliant answers!

8. Your body language should communicate confidence and sincerity.

While studies differ slightly on just what percentage of human interaction is unspoken, there is definitely consensus that it is way more than most would believe. Take advantage of this knowledge during your interview. Posture is one of our weaknesses; both of us tend to slouch forward (likely due to our larger than average height). This can give us a negative or aggressive impression—so we remind ourselves to sit up straight, which shows confidence and competence without appearing too aggressive. If you're being panel-interviewed, don't cross your hands in front of you, which many people say communicates that you want to hide something. Instead, leave your hands on the chair's armrests and situate yourself with a very open orientation to everyone at the table. Another option, one that might work best when you're dealing with only one or two interviewers, is to lean slightly forward to show engagement, though not on the edge of your seat or slumping. Basically, just consider how certain body language makes you feel if you were on the other side of the interview table. When questioned by someone, initially make eye contact; but also make sure to do so with the other interviewers, who may be paying close attention to you—because you never know who might have the most say in who gets hired.

9. Use the professional vocabulary associated with the job.

Before an interview, when you're mentally preparing (because you got there forty minutes early), it might be helpful to review some of the professional jargon of your field. This is especially true if it's your first time through the hiring-process. Confident use of appropriate vocabulary gives the impression that you are capable and knowledgeable about the job. It gives your presentation a truly professional feeling if you can "talk the talk". Of course, this doesn't mean you should try to force buzzwords awkwardly into the conversation. Just answer as you normally would; if you know the information well and have prepared properly, you should see opportunities to show off that knowledge a little.

10. Bring extra copies of your résumé.

As we stated in APPENDIX A, you should bring extra copies everywhere you go when job-hunting—especially to interviews. Start by investing in a nice briefcase: it makes a very important professional first impression and is relatively inexpensive—and setting it on the table and asking whether anyone else needs a copy of your résumé before you begin is a great way to show assertively that you are prepared for the interview. Besides a briefcase, which is relatively large, another option for presenting your résumé is an ultra-sturdy and professional-looking folder, like those in which diplomas often are presented. Projecting professionalism is the key objective no matter what option you choose. Make sure you know your résumé thoroughly and can mention it in your answers. Any confusion or mix-ups can quickly give the impression that you were not fully honest about your qualifications on the résumé.

11. If you bring a portfolio, make sure you know what you want to do with it.

In Manitoba, the academics of the teaching world are extremely high on the idea of using professional portfolios as showcases during interviews. Unfortunately, those academics have little connection to the administrators, who are uninterested in paging through an intimidating binder full of the same stuff they've just seen from the previous candidate. If you are going to bring a portfolio to a job interview, you ought to know how to use it and how to locate an item quickly while looking at it upside-down so that the person across the table can see it right-side-up. Start the interview by simply stating that you have a portfolio and that it will be coming around if anyone wants to look at it. If you want to use a document from the portfolio, put it where people can find it; that way, if they are interested, they can look at it when it comes to them.

There are many theories about portfolios, but we truly believe they are overrated. In most cases, those administrators have seen so many portfolios that they probably all blur together. The best portfolio tip Kyle got was to include pictures from all aspects of his life that he could connect to teaching. The idea behind this is to raise the chance of making the personal connection. If an interviewer is flipping through your portfolio and sees a relevant picture, that might actually stand out from the blur. In one of Kyle's interviews, he had a picture of a basketball camp he had coached at. The camp happened to be in the home town of one of the interviewers, and he was a big fan of it—cha-ching!

12. Follow up with a Thank You within twenty-four hours.

We've saved the most underrated interview tip on this list for last. If you want to stand out as the one person who really wants the job and isn't just treating the interview as another in a long line, then make sure you give a quick courtesy call or email after the interview. Just keep it short and sweet, thanking everyone for the opportunity and perhaps dropping a casual reference to something discussed in the interview (such as "Good luck with provincials this weekend" if the interviewer was a coach). Getting everyone's business card before you've left the interview will make it easy for you to reach every person who may appreciate your thanks; and, immediately after the interview, you can jot on the back of each card a note of something memorable about that person, which you can then mention in your email or phone call. Remember, people hire the candidate who thinks the most like them! Focusing on that personal connection will set you apart.

GLOSSARY

DEFINED here for your quick reference are several of the terms used in this book that may be newer to you. Words that are printed in SMALL CAPITALS within the definitions also have their own entries.

actuary. In INSURANCE, a mathematician who uses statistics to calculate the risk of a given LOSS in given circumstances.

appreciation. Growth in monetary value. Real estate often appreciates at a rate much higher than that of general INFLATION: if you buy land or a house in a growing market in one year, you may be able to sell it not many years later for much more than you bought it for, even though the prices of other goods and services in the economy have not risen as fast. The opposite of appreciation is DEPRECIATION.

beneficiary. In INSURANCE, the person who receives the BENEFIT. In scholarships, bursaries, and grants, the person who is awarded the money, which is given by the *benefactor* or *sponsor*.

benefit. The amount of money that an INSURANCE COMPANY gives to a POLICYHOLDER when a CLAIM has been filed and verified. The policyholder uses the benefit to cope with whatever LOSS resulted in the claim.

Canada Education Savings Grant (CESG). The federal government's contribution towards a student's REGISTERED EDUCATION SAVINGS PLAN.

Canada Pension Plan (CPP). The part of Canada's "social safety net" that provides continuing income for retirees. All working Canadians pay into this pool of money.

Canada Revenue Agency (CRA). The agency within the federal government that handles the collection of taxes.

claim. An application to an INSURANCE COMPANY, usually from a POLICYHOLDER, to get the BENEFIT specified in an insurance POLICY when a LOSS has occurred. The claims process involves reporting the loss, verifying ("adjusting") the loss, and writing the BENEFIT cheque.

claims adjuster. An insurance-company employee whose job is to verify the validity of a claim and write the BENEFIT cheque.

compound interest. The INTEREST that is calculated when both the original amount of money borrowed (the PRINCIPAL) and the interest that has already accrued are added together, forming a new principal, on which new interest is charged. If you borrow money at an interest rate of 24 percent per year, compounded monthly, then the 24 percent is divided by the twelve months in a year (resulting in 2 percent per month), and the amount of money that you haven't paid back is charged 2-percent interest in a given month; the sum of those two amounts (the amount you haven't paid back, and the interest charged in that month) is the new principal, on which the next month's 2-percent interest is charged. If you borrow $100 for a year and the 24-percent annual interest is compounded monthly, the amount of money you owe after twelve months is not just $124, but $126.82: it's higher because, in each new month, interest is charged not only on the original $100 but also on the interest assessed in all the previous months. If you pay back the $100 in just six months, you will pay just $112.62—paying your debts quickly is the way to avoid losing so much money to compound interest. This "snowballing" effect works against you when you borrow money—and it works for you when you make an INVESTMENT. The non-compounding type is SIMPLE INTEREST.

coverage. The type or amount (depending on context) of protection that an insurance POLICY provides. Your car-insurance policy may include liability coverage to the tune of several tens of thousands of dollars; in that case, liability is the *type* of coverage (it protects you if you are sued in connection with driving) and the several tens of thousands of dollars are the *amount* of liability coverage.

credit check. The process of learning about someone's *creditworthiness* (trustworthiness), usually in the context of borrowing money or taking another financial risk (such as renting an apartment to someone). When you try to get a loan or transact other financial business in which the other party is taking a risk, that party may check your credit—sometimes by asking other individuals, such as former employers, about you, and often by getting your written permission to get a copy of your CREDIT REPORT from a CREDIT-REPORTING AGENCY. For your protection, there are important laws about what may and may not be done in a credit check; look them up.

credit limit. The maximum amount of money that a borrower is allowed to owe to a lender at any given moment without violating the terms of the loan.

credit line. See LINE OF CREDIT.

credit rating. See CREDIT SCORE.

credit report. A detailed summary, covering several years, of a person's handling of debt, including the names of lenders, how much credit they offered, how much money the person borrowed, whether the money was paid back as agreed, and other details. A credit report is compiled by a CREDIT-REPORTING AGENCY. An extremely brief "average" of the information in your credit report is your CREDIT SCORE. There are important laws about what other people may and may not do with your credit report, how to get your own look at it and correct false information on it, etc.; look them up.

credit-reporting agency. An organization that makes, keeps, and shares CREDIT REPORTS. Also called a *credit agency*, *credit bureau*, and *credit-reporting bureau.*

credit score. A three-digit number calculated from the information in a person's CREDIT REPORT. A higher number means that the person is a lower-risk borrower, who therefore will be offered the opportunity to borrow a larger amount of money at a lower INTEREST RATE than someone with a lower score.

creditor. A lender who has not yet been paid back fully. See also DEBTOR.

debtor. A borrower who has not yet fully paid back a loan. See also CREDITOR.

deductible. The amount of money that a POLICYHOLDER must pay out of his or her own pocket, toward the cost of a LOSS, when filing an insurance CLAIM. If a loss costs $2,000 and the POLICY specifies a $500 deductible, the policyholder is responsible for the first $500 of the loss and the INSURER gives the remaining $1,500 as the BENEFIT. If the amount of the loss is less than the deductible, there may be no point in filing a claim.

default. To fail to repay a loan as agreed. If you agree to make monthly payments toward a debt you owe, and you miss one or more monthly payments, or you stop paying altogether, you are defaulting and are said to be in default.

depreciation. Reduction in monetary value. Cars depreciate rapidly: if you buy a new car for $20,000, its resale value will be less than $20,000 as soon as you drive it off the lot, and the value will continue to decline (unless the car becomes a collectible antique). The opposite of depreciation is APPRECIATION.

education tax credit. A TAX CREDIT that many Canadian students can take when filing their annual INCOME-TAX RETURNS. See also page 104.

employment insurance (EI). The part of Canada's "social safety net" that provides regular income to persons who lose their jobs through no fault of their own, until they get back on their feet. (If you voluntarily quit your job, or are fired for misconduct, you may not get EI.) The program also helps pregnant women; parents in certain circumstances; people who are sick, injured, and in quarantine; and those caring for gravely ill relatives. EI is administered by the federal government, and the benefits come from a pool of money that all working Canadians pay into.

equity. The value of a mortgaged property minus the debts associated with it. If your house could be sold for $200,000 and you owe $150,000 toward the mortgage loan that you used to buy it, you have $50,000 in equity in the house. See also MORTGAGE LOAN.

fixed interest rate. An INTEREST RATE, on a loan, that will stay the same until all the money is paid back. A fixed interest rate may be based on what the PRIME INTEREST RATE was when the loan terms were set in stone, but the loan's interest rate will not rise and fall with the continuing fluctuation of the prime rate. If you take out a loan with a five-percent fixed interest rate, you will always pay interest at five percent, no matter what the prime rate does.

Goods-and-Services Tax (GST). A TAX that the federal government charges on almost all goods and services sold in Canada. It is now five percent. If the price sticker says "$1.00", then you will pay $1.05 to buy the item and the extra 5¢ will go to the government.

grade-point average (GPA). The average of all your marks on all your assignments in a given course, or the average of all your marks in all the courses you've completed, depending on context. The latter form of GPA often is used to determine entry into faculties and to determine whether a student should be placed on academic probation. Your GPA also affects your chances of getting a scholarship: benefactors are more interested in giving money to those who do well in school.

gross. The amount or quantity of something before things are subtracted from it. If you work eight hours at a gross rate of $10 an hour, your gross earnings for those hours are $80—but you probably will not receive the full $80, because each PAYROLL DEDUCTION will reduce your NET pay.

income tax. A TAX whose amount is based on the amount of money that a person receives. If your GROSS income in a year is $100,000 and your income tax is twenty-six percent, you owe $26,000 in tax for that year. In the real world, income tax is more complicated, because not all income is taxed, and not all tax rates are the same percentage. Income tax is a form of PAYROLL TAX.

income-tax return. The form, usually filed annually with the government, that a person uses to figure out how much INCOME TAX he or she has paid, has overpaid, or still owes, to the government. Filing your return each year is important not only because it's legally required but also because, especially when you're young, it may mean that the government gives you back money that you've already paid in taxes. More and more people nowadays simplify the process of filling out their returns by using free tax software and then filing the return through NETFILE.

inflation. The increase in the number of dollars and cents that it costs to buy a given product or service. A loaf of bread made in a certain way, from certain ingredients, and of a certain weight, may have cost 30¢ in the past—and now exactly the same kind of loaf may cost $2.00, meaning the price, expressed as dollars and cents, has been inflated. Inflation is usually expressed as a percentage over a given period: if an item cost $1.00 last year and it sells for $1.03 this year, we say that it underwent three-percent annual inflation. Economists track the prices of a large range of commonly purchased goods and services and then average this gradual increase in prices into a figure that we have called *general inflation* in this book. Tuition for higher education in Canada is rising faster than the price of most other goods and services: the rate of what we call *tuition inflation* is greater than that of general inflation. Sometimes, prices, expressed as dollars and cents, shrink as time goes by; this is called *deflation*.

insurance. See pages 151–153 for a quick description of insurance and how it works. Pages 153–160 discuss car, tenant's, medical and dental, and travel insurance. The table on page 160 lists some other common types of insurance and the circumstances that they help with.

insurance agent. The middleman responsible for selling an INSURANCE COMPANY'S POLICY to a POLICYHOLDER, and sometimes for ongoing communication between the insurer and the policyholder. Some agents, working with several companies, can help the customer find the company that will be the best fit for his or her needs. Agents are also called *brokers*.

insurance broker. See INSURANCE AGENT.

insurance company. A company that creates, administers, and provides INSURANCE. Insurance companies are also called *insurance providers* and *insurers*.

insurance provider. See INSURANCE COMPANY.

insured. A person whose circumstances or possessions are insured. In many cases, the insured is the same as the POLICYHOLDER: in homeowner's insurance, for example, the policyholder (the person who owns the POLICY, pays the PREMIUM, and gets the BENEFIT in the event of a LOSS for which a CLAIM has been filed) can also be called the *insured*. In other cases, the terms *insured* and *policyholder* designate different persons: in life insurance, for example, the policyholder (who owns the policy and pays the premium) can be someone other than the insured (the person whose life is insured—the person on whose death a BENEFIT will be paid to a BENEFICIARY).

insurer. See INSURANCE COMPANY.

interest. The amount of money that is charged for the use of someone else's money. If you borrow $100 and there is interest attached to the loan, you are agreeing to pay the lender not only the original $100 (the PRINCIPAL) but also some other money (interest) to compensate the lender for the fact that he or she couldn't use his or her money while it was in your hands. Interest usually is determined by multiplying the principal by a given percentage, called the INTEREST RATE: for example, if you borrow $100 at a five-percent interest rate, you will pay $5 in interest. A common type, COMPOUND INTEREST, quickly "snowballs" the amount of money that you must pay for the privilege of borrowing money and not paying it back quickly. On the other hand, if you invest in something as simple as a savings account, you're essentially lending the bank your money—and the bank will pay you a small amount of interest for the privilege of borrowing your money, which it can lend to other account-holders, whom it will charge a higher interest rate. The longer you keep your money in the bank, the more it grows. (The rare, non-compounding type of interest is SIMPLE INTEREST.)

interest rate. A set portion or multiple by which a PRINCIPAL is multiplied to determine the amount of INTEREST; it's often expressed as a percentage. If you lend someone $100 at five-percent SIMPLE INTEREST, he or she must pay you $5 (that's five percent of the $100 PRINCIPAL) in addition to repaying the $100. In terms of constancy and flexibility, the two kinds of interest rate are the FIXED INTEREST RATE and the VARIABLE INTEREST RATE.

investment. A piece of property, or a human effort, into which someone puts money in the hope that he or she will get back, from that property or effort, more money than he or she originally invested. You might invest in a house (property) or in your own education (an effort). Investments come with the risk that the money will not be regained. As an investment, a car might be a successful investment or an unsuccessful one: at face value, a car is a bad investment, because it depreciates and does it so rapidly; but, if a car enables you to do profitable things that you could not have done as profitably without the car, and if the value of those things outweighs the cost of the car, then the car may be a wise investment. The term *investment* also describes the money that is invested.

line of credit. A bank account that allows someone to borrow money (and pay interest on the loan) as he or she needs it, up to a certain amount (the CREDIT LIMIT). A STUDENT LINE OF CREDIT usually has fairy low INTEREST RATE.

loss. In INSURANCE, the expensive loss of something valuable, whether it is property, money, a job, health, a body part, or a life. Property losses occur when property is damaged, destroyed, or stolen—and even when it is just plain lost (permanently misplaced).

market value. The money that something would be likely to fetch if it were offered for sale to a fair cross-section of society. The market value of many used objects is less than what they sold for when they were new. Your three-year-old laptop computer may have cost $700 when it was new, but now you might get only $150 if you tried to sell it used. If you have property INSURANCE that covers your small possessions where you live (a renter's-insurance policy, or contents coverage in a homeowner's-insurance policy), market-value COVERAGE will pay you only a small benefit, not enough to replace your damaged, destroyed, lost, or stolen possessions: $150, for example, won't go very far toward replacing a computer that would cost a lot more to buy new. In insurance, REPLACEMENT-COST coverage is a *much* better deal.

mortgage loan. Money that someone borrows to buy real estate. Land and buildings are so expensive that the average person would have to save money for decades in order to buy a place to live in without borrowing. Saving the money would take even longer if a big chunk of each month's paycheque had to be spent paying rent to a landlord for a dwelling—money that never provides the tenant any ownership of the dwelling (see EQUITY), just permission to stay there for another thirty days or so. That is why people are willing to borrow huge amounts of money (often well over $100,000) now and to spend many years paying it back—because it means they're building equity, ownership, in a place they can live in indefinitely, rather than paying someone else to let them stay somewhere for a month at a time. Banks are willing to lend such large sums of money partly because real estate often undergoes APPRECIATION and because borrowers are heavily invested in their homes and therefore likely to pay back the loans.

moving tax credit. A TAX CREDIT that Canadian students can take when filing their INCOME-TAX RETURNS if they moved at least 40 kilometres (by the shortest usual public route) to attend post-secondary education full time. See also page 106.

mutual fund. A type of INVESTMENT in which someone buys pieces (or units) of a large pool of money that is then handled by an investment manager, who invests the pooled money in a variety of properties and human efforts. The types of investments made by managers often carry risks that the invested money will not be regained; but it is unlikely that the *entire variety* of investments made through a mutual fund will fail—so a mutual fund is a way for someone with relatively little money to get the benefits of investing in a wider (and therefore safer) range of properties and efforts without having a lot of money.

net. The amount or quantity of something after things are subtracted from it. If you work eight hours at a GROSS rate of $10 an hour, your gross earnings for those hours are $80—but, if a PAYROLL DEDUCTION is made to your gross earnings, your net earnings will be less than $80.

NETFILE. The program that allows Canadians to submit their income-tax returns to the Canada Revenue Agency through the Internet, as opposed to the traditional method of "snail mail".

non-refundable tax credit. A TAX CREDIT that can reduce to zero the amount of INCOME TAX you owe but which cannot take that number into the negative. If you've paid $700 in income tax in a year and you're now doing your yearly INCOME-TAX RETURN, and you find that you're eligible for a $1,000 non-refundable tax credit, you will get back the $700 you paid in income tax, *but* you will not also get another $300. The reasoning "$700 minus $1,000 equals negative $300, so give me back all the $700 I paid in taxes and then give me $300 more" doesn't apply for a non-refundable tax credit.

payroll deduction. Money that is subtracted from your GROSS job earnings before the paycheque for your NET earnings is written. It is common to have PAYROLL TAX deducted immediately from gross earnings. Many people also have a portion of their gross pay set aside in RRSPs before the cheque is written for the net amount; this kind of payroll deduction comes out even before payroll taxes are assessed, meaning that fewer dollars are taken in tax from the gross pay.

payroll tax. TAX that a person must pay and which is figured as a percentage of his or her GROSS job earnings. Some common payroll taxes are INCOME TAX and payments toward the CANADA PENSION PLAN and EMPLOYMENT INSURANCE. Usually, an estimated amount of payroll tax that will be due is subtracted from your gross pay before a paycheque is even written, resulting in smaller NET pay; this payroll deduction is made automatically so that you won't spend all your gross pay and have no money left with which to pay this year's payroll taxes when it's time to pay them early next year. In some circumstances, you can request that the money not be deducted automatically from your gross pay (see page 108); you'll then have to ensure that you have set aside the amount you'll owe in taxes so that you can pay them on time next year.

peril. In INSURANCE, the cause of a LOSS or potential loss. Fire and theft are common perils in property insurance.

policy. The contract, between an INSURANCE COMPANY and a POLICYHOLDER, that describes the INSURANCE arrangement, including the BENEFICIARY, the BENEFIT, the COVERAGE, the DEDUCTIBLE, the PREMIUM, the TERM, etc.

policyholder. A person who buys a POLICY from an INSURANCE COMPANY. He or she owns the policy and pays the PREMIUM.

premium. The price that a POLICYHOLDER pays for an insurance POLICY. The premium is a set amount of money per TERM; often it can be broken up into installments paid annually, semiannually, quarterly, or monthly.

principal. The original amount of money borrowed or invested, before INTEREST accrues.

prime interest rate. (1) The INTEREST RATE set periodically by the Bank of Canada, often called the *overnight rate.* (2) The interest rate that a bank offers on loans to its lowest-risk borrowers; this rate usually is tied closely to the prime interest rate set by the Bank of Canada. Both types of prime interest rate are also called *prime, prime lending rate,* and *prime rate.* The interest rates on many kinds of loans, including car loans, lines of credit, mortgages, and student loans, are based on the prime rate.

property tax credit. A TAX CREDIT that Canadians can take when filing their INCOME TAX RETURNS if they rent or own their primary residences. See also pages 107–108.

Registered Education Savings Plan (RESP). An INVESTMENT account created to support post-secondary education. There are special tax advantages to this kind of investment. The government also offers several other perks, including the CANADA EDUCATION SAVINGS GRANT (CESG), as incentives for parents to help plan and pay for their children's education.

Registered Retirement Savings Plan (RRSP). An INVESTMENT account created to encourage saving for retirement. There are special tax advantages to this type of investment. Growth within an RRSP is not taxed; only money that is withdrawn from the account (usually when the account-holder retires) is taxed.

replacement cost. In INSURANCE, the amount of money necessary to buy a suitable replacement for an item that has been damaged, destroyed, lost, or stolen. Property-insurance policies typically offer either one of two kinds of COVERAGE: replacement cost and MARKET VALUE. Replacement-cost coverage is a *much* better deal than coverage for the mere market value of an item.

simple interest. The form of INTEREST that is not COMPOUND INTEREST. When simple interest is the name of the game (which is rare), the amount of money that the borrower must pay to the lender is the PRINCIPAL plus the interest; but, contrary to how things go with compound interest, the interest owed is not periodically added to the principal to produce a new, larger principal on which further interest is then calculated.

student line of credit (SLOC). A LINE OF CREDIT designed for students, usually with a fairy low INTEREST RATE. There are special SLOCs with very high CREDIT LIMITS for students who are studying to go into certain high-paying professions that require very expensive training and equipment, such as dentistry.

subletting. The scenario in which a tenant who has a rental contract with the landlord of an apartment or house temporarily vacates the property while the contract is still in force and then rents the space to a third party for a designated period and price while the original tenant is legally still renting from the landlord. The original tenant's contract with the real landlord often includes terms that describe the conditions under which subletting is allowed or forbidden.

T4. The main document needed to complete the average Canadian's INCOME-TAX RETURN. It explains how much money a worker earned during the previous year and how much PAYROLL TAX the employer deducted from the worker's GROSS pay before the cheque for the NET pay was written.

T4A. Similar to a T4, but specific to the income derived from annuities, pensions, retirement accounts, and certain other sources (such as scholarships, bursaries, and grants). It describes the income's source and how much INCOME TAX (if any) was deducted at the source.

T1213. A form from the Canada Revenue Agency that a taxpayer can use to request a reduction in the amount of TAX that is automatically deducted at the source of your income. For example, you can use a T1213 to make your job paycheque be closer to the full amount of your GROSS pay. This does not reduce the amount of tax that you actually *owe*; it just reduces the amount that's taken *automatically* from your income before it even lands in your hands. See also page 108.

T2202A. The TAX form of the Canada Revenue Agency used for textbook, education, and tuition TAX CREDITS when an INCOME-TAX RETURN is filed. Most post-secondary institutions now allow you to print the T2202A from your online student account.

tax. Money that individuals, companies, and other groups pay to the government so that the government has money with which to do its job. There are federal and provincial taxes. Some taxes, such as the GOODS-AND-SERVICES TAX, are charged immediately and are simple to calculate. Others, including INCOME TAX, require more complex figuring, and some are paid long after the occurrence of the transactions that necessitated them.

tax credit. A reduction in the amount of tax owed by someone who meets certain requirements, such as going to school full time. In Canada, tax credits are granted at the lowest INCOME-TAX rate, and the lowest federal income-tax rate is fifteen percent. This means that, whatever the amount of the tax credit is, it is multiplied by 0.15 to determine the amount of tax money you'll save.

tax-deductible expense. An expense that reduces the amount of your income that is subject to INCOME TAX. The government decides what expenses are deductible and to what extent. If you earn $50,000 during the year, and you spent $2,000 of that on tax-deductible expenses, you will owe income tax on just the $48,000 that you didn't spend on tax-deductible expenses.

TD1. A form that a taxpayer fills out and give to his or her employer (or another person or group that provides him or her with income) to help determine the TAX CREDITS that the taxpayer is entitled to and the TAX that should be taken automatically from the GROSS income. This can be used with a T1213. See also page 108.

term. The duration of a contract, whether it's a rental agreement for an apartment or an insurance POLICY.

textbook tax credit. A TAX CREDIT that Canadian students can take when filing their INCOME-TAX RETURNS. See also page 104.

tuition tax credit. A TAX CREDIT that Canadian students can take when filing their INCOME-TAX RETURNS. See also pages 104–105.

underwriter. The employee at an INSURANCE COMPANY who determines whether a certain POLICY can be sold to a certain customer.

variable interest rate. An INTEREST RATE that rises and falls over time, depending on the fluctuations of an underlying figure, such as the PRIME INTEREST RATE. When you hear an interest rate described as "prime plus two percent" or something similar (see pages 81–82), it means that the loan has a variable interest rate that will go up and down with the prime rate.

BIBLIOGRAPHY

ALPHABETICALLY by author, this list points you in the right direction for three kinds of articles, books, and reports that you might want to check out for yourself: works from which we got direct quotations and other specific information that appear in MORE MONEY FOR BEER AND TEXTBOOKS, works that we mentioned in passing, and works that we haven't explicitly mentioned elsewhere but do definitely recommend. Page numbers tell where in this book we mentioned the source or used information from it.

Bach, David. *Fight for Your Money: How to Stop Getting Ripped Off and Save a Fortune*. Crown Business, 2009. Bach, who gave the name "The Latte Factor" to the fortunes that people spend on frivolities in small daily amounts (p. 120), has written several good books. Among his many worth checking out are *The Automatic Millionaire: A Powerful One-Step Plan to Live and Finish Rich* (2005); *Debt Free for Life: The Finish Rich Plan for Financial Freedom* (2010); *Go Green, Live Rich: 50 Simple Ways to Save the Earth and Get Rich Trying* (2008); and *Smart Women Finish Rich: 9 Steps to Achieving Financial Security and Funding Your Dreams* (revised edition, 2002).

Bradshaw, James. "University Education No Guarantee of Earnings Success". *The Globe and Mail*, 25 September 2011: *http://www.theglobeandmail.com/news/national/education/university-education-no-guarantee-of-earnings-success/article4182805/* Our source for how long it takes to earn back money spent on university (pp. 164–165).

Carlson, Kathryn Blaze. "Today's Graduates: Too Few Jobs, Not Enough Pay". *National Post*, 11 June 2011: *http://news.nationalpost.com/2011/06/11/todays-graduates-too-few-jobs-not-enough-pay/* Our source for the quote from the San Diego State University professor (p. 172).

Canadian Federation of Independent Business. "Small Business Being Squeezed by Labour Shortages". 20 March 2012: *http://www.cfib-fcei.ca/english/article/3849-small-business-being-squeezed-by-labour-shortages.html* Our source for the report of labour as a concern facing independent businesses (p. 171).

Carnegie, Dale. *How to Win Friends and Influence People.* 1936; revised edition, 1981; Simon and Schuster, 2009. After more than seventy-five years, still a world-renowned resource for anyone, young or old, who wants to get along better with other people—at school, at home, at work, at play, and in the job market. Recommended (p. 36).

Carrick, Rob. "2012 vs. 1984: Young Adults Really Do Have It Harder Today". *The Globe and Mail,* 7 May 2012: *http://www.theglobeandmail.com/globe-investor/personal-finance/2012-vs-1984-young-adults-really-do-have-it-harder-today/article4105604/* Our source for both mentions of Carrick on p. 11.

———. *How Not to Move Back In with Your Parents: The Young Person's Complete Guide to Financial Empowerment.* Doubleday Canada, 2012. Mentioned by name (p. 166).

Certified General Accountants Association of Canada. *Youth Unemployment in Canada: Challenging Conventional Thinking?* October 2012: *http://www.cga-canada.org/en-ca/ResearchAndAdvocacy/AreasofInterest/Employment/Pages/ca_employment.aspx* Cited by name (pp. 165, 168).

Chilton, David. *The Wealthy Barber: Everyone's Common-Sense Guide to Becoming Financially Independent.* Prima Lifestyles, 1991. Recommended (p. 178).

———. *The Wealthy Barber Returns: Dramatically Older and Marginally Wiser, David Chilton Offers His Unique Perspectives on the World of Money.* Financial Awareness Corporation, 2011. Recommended (p. 178).

Friese, Lauren. "Why Are We Training Our Arts Grads to Be Baristas?" *The Globe and Mail,* 29 August 2012: *http://www.theglobeandmail.com/report-on-business/economy/canada-competes/why-are-we-training-our-arts-grads-to-be-baristas/article4507579/* Our source for the Adelle Farrelly quotations (p. 166) and the quotation beginning "Students need to step up" (p. 174).

Hallam, Andrew. *The Millionaire Teacher: The Nine Rules of Wealth You Should Have Learned in School.* Wiley, 2011. Recommended (p. 178).

Holman, Mike. *The RESP Book: The Simple Guide to Registered Education Savings Plans for Canadians.* Money Smarts Publishing, 2010. Recommended (pp. 65, 66, 106).

Human Resources and Skills Development Canada. "The Canada Student Loans Program". 27 August 2009: *http://www.hrsdc.gc.ca/eng/learning/canada_student_loan/cslp.shtml* Our source for the history of Canada student loans (p. 70).

Lewington, Jennifer. "Will an Undergrad Degree Really Help You Get a Better Job?". *The Globe and Mail*, 23 October 2011: *http://www.theglobeandmail.com/news/national/education/will-an-undergrad-degree-really-help-you-get-a-better-job/article601007/* Our source for the difference in average lifetime earnings, and job losses and gains, between those with and without certain post-secondary credentials (p. 13).

Macdonald, David; Erika Shaker. *Eduflation and the High Cost of Learning*. Canadian Centre for Policy Alternatives, 11 September 2012: *http://www.policyalternatives.ca/sites/default/files/uploads/publications/National%20Office/2012/09/Eduflation%20and%20High%20Cost%20Learning.pdf* Our source for tuition inflation since 1990 and projected tuition in 2015 (p. 11).

Maclean's Magazine Editorial Team. *Maclean's: 2012 Guide to Canadian Universities*. Rogers Publishing, 2012. A useful resource on most of Canada's universities.

Mangaroo, Kelvin. "Back to School Reality CHEQUE". *Money Wise* blog, 4 September 2012: *http://www.ratesupermarket.ca/blog/back-to-school-reality-cheque* Our source for the costs of different educational options (p. 8; we graphed the information and broke it down by year, month, week, and workday on p. 10).

ManpowerGroup. *2012 Talent Shortage Survey Research Results*. 2012?: *http://www.manpowergroup.us/campaigns/talent-shortage-2012/pdf/2012_Talent_Shortage_Survey_Results_US_FINALFINAL.pdf* Our source for the Manpower global survey (p. 171).

Marshall, Katherine. "Employment Patterns of Postsecondary Students". *Perspectives on Labour and Income*, 11:9 (September 2010): *http://www.statcan.gc.ca/pub/75-001-x/2010109/article/11341-eng.htm* Mentioned by name (pp. 93–94).

Matthews, Gail. "Goals Research Summary". 2008: *http://www.dominican.edu/academics/ahss/undergraduate-programs-1/psych/faculty/fulltime/gailmatthews/researchsummary2.pdf* Our source for Dr. Matthews's study (pp. 114–115).

Ontario College of Teachers. *Transition to Teaching 2010: Early-Career Teachers in Ontario Schools*. February 2011: *http://www.oct.ca/~/media/PDF/Transition%20to%20Teaching%202010/EN/2011%20T2T%20Report%20EN%20ACCESSIBLE%20WEB.ashx* Our source for the number of unemployed and underemployed OCT graduates (p. 168).

Prairie Research Associates. "Graduating Students Survey". Unpublished, 2009. Cited on p. 115 of Joseph Berger, Anne Motte, and Andrew Parkin, editors, *The Price of Knowledge: Access and Student Finance in Canada*, 4th edition, published by The Canada Millennium Scholarship Foundation, 2009. Our source for the carried monthly credit-card balance of the average Canadian graduating from university (p. 137).

Pyper, Wendy. "Skilled Trades Employment". *Perspectives on Labour and Income*, 9:10 (October 2008): *http://www.statcan.gc.ca/pub/75-001-x/2008110/article/10710-eng.htm* Our source for the hourly average wage in the skilled trades (p. 171).

Ramsey, Dave. *Financial Peace: Restoring Financial Hope to You and Your Family*. Viking, 1997. This resource has helped countless people end their struggles with debt—victoriously. Also check out his *Financial Peace Revisited* (2002) and *Dave Ramsey's Complete Guide to Money: The Handbook of Financial Peace University* (2012).

Sethi, Ramit. *I Will Teach You to Be Rich: No Guilt. No Excuses. No B.S. Just a 6-Week Program That Works*. Workman Publishing Company, 2009. Mentioned by name (p. 35).

Skills Canada; Canadian Apprenticeship Forum. *Backgrounder: Skilled Trades: A Career You Can Build On*. August 2004: *http://www.caf-fca.org/files/Awareness_Perception_Study_Highlights_Eng.pdf* Our source for the Ipsos Reid survey (p. 171).

Taylor, Timothy. "Are Student Loans the Next Financial Bubble?" *The Globe and Mail*, 29 September 2011: *http://www.theglobeandmail.com/report-on-business/rob-magazine/are-student-loans-the-next-financial-bubble/article596063/* Our source for the amount of outstanding student-loan debt (p. 12).

TD Canada Trust. "TD Canada Trust 2011 Report on Savings: 54% of Canadians Struggle to Save". 20 April 2011: *http://www.smrmediaroom.ca/TDSavings.html* Our source for the portion of Canadians who make only the minimum required payments toward their credit-card debt (p. 137).

Waisberg, Deena. "How Your Kids Can Get a Scholarship". *Canadian Living*, September 2008: *http://www.canadianliving.com/life/money/how_your_kids_can_get_a_scholarship.php* Our source for the amount of unclaimed scholarship money (p. 29).

CPSIA information can be obtained at www.ICGtesting.com
Printed in the USA
LVOW051725230513

335256LV00005B/494/P